M000234795

REPORT OF THE COMMISSION

TO

Investigate and Report the Most Humane and Practical Method

OF

CARRYING INTO EFFECT

THE

Sentence of Death in Capital Cases.

ELBRIDGE T. GERRY,
ALFRED P. SOUTHWICK, } *Commissioners.*
MATTHEW HALE,

TRANSMITTED TO THE LEGISLATURE, JANUARY   1888.

REPORT OF THE COMMISSION

TO

Investigate and Report the Most Humane and Practical Method

OF

CARRYING INTO EFFECT

THE

Sentence of Death, in Capital Cases.

ELBRIDGE T. GERRY,
ALFRED P. SOUTHWICK, } *Commissioners.*
MATTHEW HALE,

TRANSMITTED TO THE LEGISLATURE, JANUARY 17, 1888.

THE TROY PRESS COMPANY, PRINTERS.

1888.

STATE OF NEW YORK.

IN SENATE,

JANUARY 17, 1888.

REPORT

OF THE

COMMISSION TO INVESTIGATE AND REPORT THE MOST HUMANE AND PRACTICAL METHOD OF CARRYING INTO EFFECT THE SENTENCE OF DEATH IN CAPITAL CASES.

To the Legislature of the State of New York:

The commission appointed (by Laws of 1886, chapter 352, extended by Laws of 1887, chapter 7) "to investigate and report at an early date the most humane and practical method known to modern science of carrying into effect the sentence of death in capital cases," respectfully report:

First. Immediately after their appointment your commission met and carefully considered the general outlines of the subject, and also examined the entire criminal law from its earliest history down to the present time, as to the principles upon which the infliction of capital punishment was based, the methods of execution and the reasons therefor. And in order that the conclusions at which your commission have arrived may be fully understood, they respectfully submit the following.

HISTORY OF THE LAW.

Capital punishment has two objects in view, first the deprivation of the life of the criminal as a punishment for his crime and because its continuance would be fraught with danger to the State; second by deterrent effects resulting from the punishment to warn other evil-minded and dangerous persons in the community that a similar violation of the law will result in equally fatal consequences to themselves, and thus to lessen the commission of crime in the future.

The early history of the criminal law shows a general attempt to check the increase of crime by making the punishment for a large number of offenses a capital one. Thus, for instance, under the Mosaic law, many offenses were punished capitally, as being violations of the national faith, a very full and complete list of which [1] is as follows:

CAPITAL PUNISHMENT IN THE MOSAIC CODE.

Murder	Exod.	xxi, 12
Kidnapping	Exod.	xxi, 16
Eating leavened bread during the passover	Exod.	xii, 15
Suffering an unruly ox to be at liberty, if he kill, (the ox also to be stoned)	Exod.	xxi, 29
Witchcraft	Exod.	xxii, 18
Bestiality (the beast put to death)	Exod.	xxii, 19
Idolatry	Exod.	xxii, 20
Oppression of widow and fatherless	Exod.	xxii, 22
Compounding holy ointment or putting it on any stranger	Exod.	xxx, 33
Violation of the Sabbath	Exod.	xxxi, 14
Smiting of one's father or mother	Exod.	xxi, 15
Sodomy	Lev.	xx, 13
Eating the flesh of the sacrifice of peace offerings with uncleanness	Lev.	vii, 20
Eating the fat of offered beasts	Lev.	vii, 25
Eating any manner of blood	Lev.	vii, 27
Offering children to Moloch	Lex.	xx, 2
Eating a sacrifice of peace-offering	Lev.	xix, 8
Screening an idolator	Lev.	xx, 4
Going after familiar spirits and wizards	Lev.	xx, 6
Adultery (both parties, if female married, and not a bond-maid)	Lev.	xx, 10
Incest (three kinds)	Lev.	xx, 11
Cursing of parents	Lev.	xx, 9
Unchastity in priest's daughter	Lev.	xxi, 9

[1] Spear on Capital Punishment, p. 159.

The Athenian code of laws established by Draco[1] prescribed the punishment of death for a large number of offenses, greatly differing in degrees of criminality, which the law-giver extenuated by saying that the smallest of the crimes specified deserved death, and there was no greater penalty which he could inflict for more heinous offenses. This severity was afterwards very much modified, and the Athenian criminal code became very mild, subject, however, to an arbitrary power reserved to the assembly of the people over the lives of all the citizens, and also to a discretion, which in many instances was left to the areopagus, and even to the dicasts of the people, of determining the punishment as well as the guilt of the accused; as in the case of Socrates, who, after trial by the court of areopagus was retried with reference to the punishment. It was generally in the power of an Athenian to escape from a trial, if he was unwilling to incur the risk, by going into voluntary exile. Arrest before trial was not the practice in judicial proceedings, either civil or criminal, in the Athenian courts The crimes ordinarily punished by death, or for which death was prescribed by law, were sacrilege, impiety (any open disrespect for religious rites or popular faith), treason, murder, or the attempt to murder, and incendiarism.

The grievous tendency toward an unnecessary multiplication of capital crimes which prevailed during earlier periods of English history is well known. There are said to have been in England at the time when criminal jurisprudence in this country was forming, about 100 different offenses which had been declared felonies, and

---

[1] American Cyclopedia, p. 754.

might (except for the contention of some humane lawyers that felony was not in all cases capital, and for the amelioration of the death penalty introduced by the privilege of benefit of clergy), be punished with death. It was found, however, that the application of the severe sentence of the death penalty to the minor offenses did not practically check their commission. And in modern times, by the repeal of these various statutes, the death penalty is now universally limited to cases of treason, murder, piracy, military offenses, and crimes involving the greatest injury to the individual upon whom they are perpetrated, or the community in which they are committed.

The following account of the condition of affairs which prevailed in England during the closing years of the eighteenth century, and of the legislative reform which then began and which culminated in 1832,[1] will convey a graphic view of this subject.

Capital punishment continued to be a public exhibition long after the pillory ceased to be used, and from the time of the revolution until nearly the middle of the present century there is an aspect of it which claims attention, even before its hardening effect upon the spectators. This is its indiscriminate application. With the development of new industries and the new facilities for commerce, new frauds became possible, and the ordinary mode of dealing with them by statute was to declare them felonies, either with or without benefit of clergy. It was a maxim with some lawyers, that although felony implied forfeiture, it was not necessarily followed by death. As a matter of fact, however, hanging was a part of the punishment for felony. The number of offenses to which capital punishment was applicable continued to increase year by year in proportion to the increase in the number of conceivable offenses against property. In earlier times it was impossible to counterfeit tickets in lotteries which had no existence, to forge the seal or the notes of the bank of England, which was not established, to personate the holder of a stock and transfer it, or receive the dividends due upon it, when it was not yet created, or to make a malicious attack upon a turnpike which had not yet been built. It was strictly in accordance with analogy that such acts as these were made punishable to the same extent as larceny above the value of one shilling. Perpetrators of . the greatest frauds enjoyed in earlier times a comparative impunity, while persons guilty of an inconsiderable theft were hanged. One

---

[1]Pike, History of Crime in England, 447.

reason was that trade and its devices for its propagation were continually outgrowing the primitive laws of an uncivilized people. The thief atoned for his crime with his life in accordance with ancient custom ; the forger and the swindler eluded the law, and if they suffered at all, suffered an imprisonment of which the legality was doubtful, or were set in the pillory.

The extension of the list of felonies in the eighteenth century was thus, in one aspect, a sign of progress. It indicated an attempt to inflict punishment in proportion to the heinousness of the crime. The effort, indeed, was made in the wrong direction, and frustrated itself by the inconsistencies to which it led. Not only at the end of the eighteenth century, but during a considerable portion of the nineteenth, the criminal law was more open to reproach than perhaps at any period in the history of England. In times when men had barely realized to themselves the idea of property, it was natural that (apart from religion) theft and homicide should be practically the only two forms of crime, that there should be little distinction between them, and that where a distinction was admitted, theft should be considered the greater. It was no less natural that as the nation advanced, the punishment for all the offenses against property should be made the same as that for greater larceny. But as respect for human life, together with a general widening of human sympathy, has been a part of human progress no less than the accumulation of wealth, the changes of the law suggested at first by a sense of justice, were seen to be, if logical when regarded from one point of view, both cruel and unjust when regarded from another.

When human blood was held cheap—not only figuratively but literally — when it had a fixed price in cattle or money there was no inconsistency in the fact that a murderer should buy back his life, though a thief without the means of making restitution was hanged. The extension of capital punishment to a murderer without the option of a fine was, like its extension to great and new frauds, a sign of civilization. There may seem to be a paradox in the assertion that a regard for human life is shown in condemning a human being to death for an offense for which the payment of a sum of money had previously been considered a sufficient atonement. But if a punishment be considered a deterrent, and if hanging be a greater punishment than the loss of a certain amount of property, it is clear that some attempt to give security to the person was made when the "were" was abolished. On the other hand, any value which the fear of the gallows may have possessed as a deterrent was greatly diminished, so far as homicide was concerned, by the indiscriminate use of it in relation to offenses of a very different character. When the criminal might be executed for stealing a sheep as well as for murder, he had not the slightest inducement to refrain from murder if he was detected in the act of carrying off the sheep. Nor was this the worst effect of the criminal law as it existed in the eighteenth century. Not only the thief caught in the act of theft, and with the instinct of self-preservation brought strongly into action, but persons the least criminally disposed, with ample leisure for reflection, were necessarily affected by the nominal sentiment (as expressed in the national laws) that it was no greater crime to kill a fellow Englishman than to pick a pocket.

The wise and just and benevolent men who set themselves to the work of devising a new scale of punishments could not command a great success while the military spirit was so predominant as it was before the peace of 1818. The lust of conquest is inconsistent with a high regard for human life. The failure of 1770 was followed by a very small victory in 1808, when a law was passed by which pocket-picking ceased to be a capital offense. Sir Samuel Romilly, by whose efforts this change had been effected, attempted, in 1810, to carry other similar bills, but in vain. In 1811, however, his bill for withdrawing the offense of stealing from bleaching-grounds out of the list of crimes punishable with death, passed both houses, and in 1812 a bill of his relating to soldiers and sailors found begging. In 1813, 1816 and 1818 he introduced a bill to abolish capital punishment for stealing to the value of five shillings from shops. As in 1810, he found support in the House of Commons, but not in the House of Lords; and when he died men could still be hanged for stealing good s of very small value from dwelling-houses, shops or river craft.

With the firm establishment of peace, however, a more merciful public opinion began to assert itself in no faltering language. 'Sir James Mackintosh was a worthy successor to Sir Samuel Romilly within the House of Commons, and was effectively supported by the popular voice without. Many petitions were presented, and in 1819 a committee of the Commons was appointed to report upon capital punishments. In 1820 Mackintosh succeeded in changing the law so far that it was no longer a capital offense to steal from a shop unless to the value of fifteen pounds. He also gained a triumph rather apparent than real in abolishing capital punishment as applied to a

number of crimes which were nearly obsolete or of very rare occurrence. Various other efforts were also made in the same direction,
but with little real success until 1832.

Until that year horse stealing, cattle stealing, stealing from a
dwelling-house, and forgery in general were capital offenses. From
that time forward none of them were capital except forgery of wills
and of powers of attorney to transfer stock. House breaking ceased
to be capital in 1833, returning from transportation (before the term
of sentence had expired) in 1834, sacrilege and letter stealing in 1835.
Soon afterwards Lord John Russell still further reduced the list of
capital offenses; and murder, though not the only crime legally punishable with death, came to be regarded as practically the only crime
for which death was inflicted. Even a well-established attempt to
murder, if unsuccessful, was not usually followed by the extreme
penalty, so lenient did the law become in its administration as well as
in its ordinances before the year 1861. According to statutes then
passed, actual murder is now the only offense (except treason) for
which sentence of death may be pronounced.

Meantime a development of a similar reform was proceeding somewhat more easily and rapidly in the American Colonies.[1]

When our country was first settled, there were many more capital
and infamous punishments than exist at present; probably because
our ancestors came from a country in which these were very numerous.
Sometime since there were no less than 160 different offenses in England made felony, and without benefit of clergy. In Massachusetts
Colony, about A. D. 1650, there were seventeen crimes at least, punished capitally, to wit: idolatry, witchcraft, blasphemy, murder, man-
slaughter, poisoning, bestiality, sodomy, adultery, man-stealing, false
witness, treason, cursing and smiting parents, rebellious and stubborn
sons, rape, Quakers returning and Jesuits returning; and the same in
Connecticut and New Plymouth. In Massachusetts, in the year 1790,
there were but seven, to wit: Treason, murder, rape, sodomy, robbery,
burglary and arson, including only four of the said seventeen; and
since, only part of these crimes are capitally punished. So punishments were varied in other respects; the pillory, gallows, whipping
and branding almost disappeared, and solitary imprisonment and hard
labor in State prisons generally substituted in their place, as, also,
much in the place of capital punishments.

---

[1] 6 Dane's Abridgment, 637.

"Some years ago," says a recent writer,[1] "more than 200 offenses
were punishable with death. A bloody and horrible system of law
grew up chiefly since the revolution of 1688, and during the time the
present family have been on the throne of this country — and we have
been under the government of an aristocracy assumed to be very
enlightened, and a government much more free than we had before
the revolution — more than 200 offenses, such as the stealing of a
fowl, or of five shillings worth out of a shop, were punishable with
death. Only conceive how perverted men's minds must have become
by this common custom of hanging, to tolerate such things. I recol-
lect hearing of a case of a woman whose husband had been kidnapped
by the press-gang, and she stole something from a shop in Ludgate-hill.
Well, for the sake of example, and to preserve the property of Ludgate-hill shopkeepers, she was hanged, and nobody at the time was
shocked at the matter. For the issuing of a bad half crown, or a bad
pound note, persons were in Newgate in great numbers, and out of
twenty or thirty convicted, the custom was to select a certain number,
three or four, or eight or ten, and doom them to the gallows. This
was common, at that time, in London, and the great statesmen of that
generation scarcely ever asked whether this horrible custom might
not be mitigated or abolished. The world, however, was not all in
that darkness. There was one country in the world where the law
was not so brutal, a great country on the other side of the Atlantic,
springing up from colonies founded by ourselves. In the year 1675,
William Penn founded the State of Pennsylvania, that is, in the reign
of Charles II. Consider how long ago that is. Now, we are accustomed to fancy that we have made prodigious strides in science and
everything else since that time, but when William Penn drew up the
laws of Pennsylvania, assisted by the great and good men who were
his helpers, they did not carry with them the 200 capital offenses we
had here, but struck them all out, with the exception of one, that
being the one we are now chiefly discussing, namely capital punishment for murder. They retained that punishment for only aggravated
cases of murder."

It is evident that the former policy of multiplying capital offenses
may have had a tendency to promote the employment of numerous
modes of inflicting death. Thus where several crimes of different
grades of guilt are to be so punished, it may be natural to choose
more painful and shameful modes as more appropiate to the more
heinous offenses. An illustration of this inclination to intensify the

[1] 9 Jour. Physiolg. Med., 25.

death penalty proportionately to the degree of guilt, is presented by the former English law of executions for treason.[1]

The judgment of high treason for a man in all cases, except counterfeiting the coin, was to be drawn upon a hurdle to the place of execution, there to be hanged by the neck, to be cut down while he is alive, and his entrails taken out and burned before his face; and his head to be cut off, and body quartered, and the head and quarters to be at the king's disposal. In the entry of the judgment in treason it is only said, that he shall be drawn to the place of execution, without adding "upon a hurdle," though it ought to be so pronounced; and thus it was pronounced by Holt, C. J., in the case of James Boucher, 27th February, 2 Ann. In the same case he also pronounced the judgment, that his privy members should be cut off. This ought also to be omitted in the entry of the judgment, and both these things were omitted in the entry of the judgment against Boucher by the opinion of all the judges of England. And Holt, C. J., there produced the records of the judgment against Somerville and Arden, in the time of Queen Elizabeth, and against Sir Walter Raleigh, which accorded therewith. And he said that those words, that the privy members should be cut off, were not in any records that he had seen but those in the case of the regicides. Nor indeed are they usually pronounced. For women the judgment was always the same in all cases of treason, whether high or petty treason, namely, to be drawn to the place of execution and there burned alive; but that is now altered to being drawn and hanged, by the statute, 30 Geo., 3, c. 48, s. 1 ; and by section 4, the like forfeitures and corruption of blood shall ensue as before the act. And by section 2, women convicted as principals or accessories before in petty treason, shall be liable to the further punishment inflicted by the statute, 25 Geo. 2, c. 37, on persons convicted of murder. In all cases of treason respecting the coin, whether newly created such or not, and so in petty treason, the judgment is only to be drawn on a hurdle and hanged ; for that was the judgment before the statute, 25 Ed. 3, st. 5, c. 2, and was not intended to be altered thereby ; and these being all offenses *in pari materia*, and auxiliary to the original law, have the same judgment. And such it seems was formerly the judgment for counterfeiting the great or privy seal; but now that is the same as in other treasons.

---

[1] East's Pleas of the Crown, 137.

Again,[1] the judgment in petit treason was the same as in the lower species of treason before considered, namely, to be drawn on a hurdle and hanged until dead. The judgment in murder was the same as in other cases of capital felony, namely, to be hanged by the neck until dead. But by the statute, 25 Geo. 2, c. 37, in order to stigmatize and deter persons from the commission of this heinous offense, it is enacted "that all persons who shall be found guilty of willful murder be executed according to law, on the next day but one after sentence passed (unless it happen to be Sunday, and then on the Monday following)." And (by s. 2) "the body of such murderer so convicted shall, if such conviction and execution shall be in the county of Middlesex, or within the city or liberties of London, be immediately conveyed by the sheriff, etc., to the hall of the Surgeons' Company, or such other place as the said company shall appoint, for this purpose, and to be delivered to such person as the said company shall appoint, who shall give the sheriff, etc., a receipt for the same ; and the body so delivered shall be dissected and anatomized by the said surgeons, etc. And in case such conviction and execution shall be in other county or place in Great Britain, then the judge or justice of assize or other proper judge shall award the sentence, to be put in execution the next day but one after such conviction (except as aforesaid) ; and the body of such murderer shall in like manner be delivered by the sheriff to such surgeon as such judge or justice shall direct for the purpose aforesaid." And (by s. 3) "the sentence shall be pronounced in open court immediately after the conviction of such murderer, unless the court shall see reasonable cause for postponing the same. In which sentence shall be expressed, not only the usual judgment of death, but also the time appointed thereby for the execution thereof, and the marks of infamy directed for such offenders." Section 4 enables the judge for reasonable cause to stay execution ; "regard being always had to the true intent and purpose of this act." By section 6 "such judge or justice may appoint the body of any such criminal to be hung in chains. But in no case whatever, the body of any murderer shall be suffered to be buried, unless after such body shall have been dissected and anatomized as aforesaid. And such judge or justice shall, and he is hereby required to direct the same either to be disposed of as aforesaid, to be anatomized, or to be hung in chains, in the same manner as is now practiced," etc. At a

---

[1] Page 372.

meeting of the judges in June, 1752, to consider of this law, in the case of Swan and Jefferys, they agreed that this should be the sentence or judgment: "That you be taken from hence to the prison from whence you came, and that you be taken from thence on the day of   instant (or next) to the place of execution, and that you there be hanged by the neck till your body be dead; and that your body when dead be taken down and be dissected and anatomized." They also resolved that the judgment for dissecting and anatomizing, and touching the time of execution, ought to be pronounced in cases of petit treason, though murder only is mentioned, and in that case, too, the time of execution to be a part of the judgment. There was some doubt whether either judgment of dissection or hanging in chains might not be given; and if the first were pronounced, whether if no surgeon would take the body it might not be hung in chains. But on debate it was agreed by nine judges, that in all cases within the act the judgment for dissecting and anatomizing only should be part of the judgment pronounced; and, if it were thought advisable, the judge might afterwards direct the hanging in chains by special order to the sheriff, pursuant to the proviso for that purpose in the statute: and so is the practice."

The subject of subsequent dissection of the body of the criminal as a deterrent effect will be more fully considered later.

Upon the other hand, the policy of limiting the death penalty to a very small number of crimes, which has now been the policy of this State in common with the other States and England for nearly a century, favors the idea of choosing some single simple mode of executing the sentence.

Various Modes of Capital Punishment which have been Used.

Almost all primitive forms of capital punishment, indeed the remark is true of all early punishments, are characterized by cruelty. The desire to reform the offender, to protect society from repetitions of the offense, or even to obtain redress or compensation for the wrong done, are but feebly shown in most forms of penalty which the past history of the world discloses. They all express simply an intense desire to wreak vengeance; a passionate desire to inflict physical pain and suffering, even the utmost agony possible, upon the criminal; in the belief, apparently, that by so doing society will instill terror into the hearts of evil-doers who may be tempted to commit like offenses. The modern idea of the grounds and uses of the death penalty admits, nay urges, dealing humanely with the individual, and refraining from superadding to the single, solemn fact·of death, features of the mode employed which merely intensify the suffering and heighten the shame of the culprit. Your commission have examined with care the accounts which exist of the various curious modes of capital punishment which are, or in times past have been, used among different communities with the result of feeling that the element of barbarous cruelty is so prominent in each that no existing mode can be considered as embodying suggestions of improvement in that now in use in this State. Any change, to deserve consideration, must be to a system substantially new; and the careful reader of the following descriptions of punishment cannot without prejudice, arrive at a different conclusion.

(1.) *Auto da fè.*—This name, meaning "act of faith," characterized the public executions of the persons condemned to death, upon trial and sentence, by the Spanish Inquisition. (See Burning.)

(2.) *Beating with clubs.*—This primitive, simple mode of inflicting the death penalty is said to have been in use, from very early times, among South African tribes, particularly the Hottentots. When an offense was committed, for which usage (for these people were not governed by formal written laws), prescribed death as an appropriate penalty, the culprit was seized by order of the chief of the tribe, the Kraal or village was convened, and the prisoner environed by a circle of the leading men, who, after the chief had stricken the first blow, were accustomed to rush around the victim and with their clubs end his life. Beating to death was also[1] a Greek punishment for slaves. It was inflicted on a wooden frame, which probably derived its name from resembling a drum or timbrel in form, on which the criminal was bound and beaten to death. In Josephus the same instrument was called a wheel. Hence, "to beat upon the tympanum," "to drum to death," is an expression similar to "breaking on the wheel."

(3.) *Beheading: Decapitation.*—This punishment[2] is of very ancient date and certainly known among the Greek and Romans. Xenophon says that losing the head was looked upon as the most honorable death. The decollation, as it is called, of St. John the Baptist shows the existence of this punishment among the Jews, under the Roman governor of Judea. Suetonius tells that Caligula kept a-soldier, an artist in beheading, who decapitated prisoners in his presence, fetched

---

[1] Kitto's Encyclopedia, vol. 3, p. 615.   [2] 7 Penny Encyclopedia, p. 341.

indiscriminately for that purpose from the gaols. Hoveden and Florence, of Worcester, agree that Earl Waltheof, beheaded by William the Conqueror in 1075, was the first Englishman who suffered that punishment. The Messrs. Lysons speak of beheading as an ordinary punishment in old time, of felons, in Cheshire. They say, "An ancient MS., relating to the Earls of Chester, informs us that the sergeants and bailiffs under the earls had power to behead any malefactor or thief who was apprehended in the act, or against whom guilt was proved by sufficient evidence or confession before four inhabitants of the four neighboring towns." It appears that the beheading of malefactors was the usual mode of executing in England for in a roll of Edward II. it is called the custom of Cheshire. In France criminals capitally convicted are beheaded, not hanged.

At a somewhat latter period decapitation became a punishment more especially appropriated to the higher orders of society. Henry VIII beheaded two of his queens. Elizabeth beheaded a sister sovereign and the cases of Sir Thomas More, the Earl of Essex and Sir Walter Raleigh are too familiar to need comment. The High Court of Justice beheaded Charles I. Algernon Sydney afterwards suffered the same fate. In 1644 Archbishop Laud was condemned by the two Houses of Parliament to suffer death by hanging, and the only favor granted to him on supplication, after delay and with reluctance, was that his sentence should be changed to beheading. Losing the head still continues to be considered the most honorable mode of receiving capital punishment in England, but there has been no recent instances of its having been inflicted. The last was in the case of the rebel lords of 1745.

The mode formerly practiced in England, by the ax and block, and that which originated in France late in the seventeenth century, and was gradually adopted in many other European countries—the guillotine—are described more in detail elsewhere. (See Guillotine.)

Among the Chinese[1] beheading or decapitation has always been a mode of inflicting capital punishment, but the manner of administering it differs from that common in European countries. The criminal is carried to the place of execution in a bamboo cage, and by his side is a basket in which his head will drop when removed. He is pinioned in a very effective manner. The middle of a long thin rope is passed across the back of the neck, and the ends are crossed on his chest and

---

[1] Leslie's Popular Monthly for March, 1886, p. 343.

brought under the arms. They are then twisted round the arms, the wrist tied together behind the back, and the ends fastened to the portion of the rope on the back. A slip of paper containing his name, crime and sentence is fixed to a reed and fastened at the back of his head. On arriving at the place of execution, the officials remove the paper and take it to the presiding mandarin, who writes on it in red ink, the warrant for execution. The paper is then replaced, a rope loop is passed over the head of the culprit, and the end given to an assistant, who draws the head forward so as to stretch the neck, while a second assistant holds the body from behind, and in a moment the head is severed from the body. The instrument is a sword made expressly for that purpose. It is a two-handed weapon, very heavy, and has a very broad blade. The executioners pride themselves on their dexterity in its management. After the execution, the culprit's head is taken away, and generally hung up in a bamboo cage near the scene of the crime, and with a label bearing the name and offense of the criminal. In some cases neither ropes nor assistants are required at executions, the Chinese having very little fear of death; so little, indeed, that cases have been known in which criminals have purchased substitutes for capital punishment.

Another account[1] says that in beheading, as there practiced, the malefactor is made to kneel upon the ground, the "board of infamy" is taken from his back, and the executioner, by a single blow of a two-handed sword, strikes off his head with great dexterity. These headsmen, and indeed the generality of inferior officers of justice in China are selected from the soldiery according to the custom of primitive barbarians; neither is this employment considered more ignominious than the post of principal officer of executive justice in other countries. Decapitation is held by the Chinese as the most disgraceful kind of death, because the head, which is the principal part of a man, is separated from the body, and that body is not consigned to the grave as entire as he received it from his parents. If a great mandarin be convicted of any atrocious offense, he is executed in this manner like the meanest person. After the head is severed it is frequently suspended from a tree by the side of a public road; the body is thrown into a ditch, the law having deemed it unworthy the respect of regular funeral rites. When the sentence is submitted to the emperor for his approbation, if the crime

---

[1] Punishments of China, London, 1801.

be of the first degree of atrocity, he orders the malefactor to be executed without delay; when it is only of an ordinary nature he directs that the criminal shall be imprisoned until the autumn and then executed; a particular day of that season being allotted for such ceremonies. The emperor seldom orders a subject to be executed until he has consulted with his first law officers whether he can avoid it without infringing on the constitution of his realm. He fasts for a certain period previous to signing an order for an execution; and his imperial majesty esteems those years of his reign the most illustrious and most fortunate in which he has had the least occasion to let fall upon his subjects the rigorous sword of justice.

And in the Taeping rebellion,[1] Commissioner Yeh being in authority, prisoners were taken to Canton, the Aceldama of the time, and there decapitated in gangs, a hundred, perhaps, on a morning. The culprits having been disposed side to side and face down, the executioner, preceded by an assistant to steady the head by seizing the pig-tail, moved along the line, averaging but five seconds at most to each man, and rarely making a miss.

A recent writer,[2] who considered simple beheading, as practiced in Japan, a speedier and more merciful method than the gallows, gives the following description of one witnessed by him :

" When within about half a mile of the prison we met an immense crowd of people, and on inquiry found that the criminal was even then being paraded on horseback through the town, and would pass us on his way to the place of execution. Remaining where we were we soon saw the cortege approaching. First of all came two men bearing placards raised on poles — the one proclaiming the nature of the crime for which the offender was to suffer and the punishment he was condemned to undergo, the other inscribed with his name and native place. Immediately following, guarded by two spearmen, rode the doomed man, tied to his horse, with his arms tightly pinioned behind him, and a rope fastened to his waist. This was held by a man who walked alongside. With a skin blanched, parched and shriveled, features worn and distorted, eye-balls glazed and sunk, his cheek-bones appearing to be forcing themselves out, and his withered arms hanging nerveless at his side, the wretched being strove hard to bear himself bravely, and to behave at the last as became one of his race. As he passed his eye lit on our party, and he called out, with a

---

[1] Medico Legal Papers, 2d ser., p. 260.   [2] Harper's Magazine, vol. 39, p. 310.

scornful laugh, for the foreigners to come and see how a Nippon could die.

"Next in order in the procession came some men on foot, and lastly two officers on horseback with their retainers. Following them we soon reached and were admitted into the prison. Built entirely of wood, it consisted of a collection of low, black, one-storied edifices, whose dismal hue and somber aspect alone must have been enough to crush out hope from the hearts of the unfortunates entering there. In the center of these was the court-yard or execution ground, the whole being contained within a high wooden paling. The different cells were all open on one side, and crossed and recrossed by stout wooded bars, through which you could look upon the occupants.

"Some of these — probably suffering for lesser crimes — seemed tolerably well cared for; while others, huddled together like sheep in a pen, appeared worn and emaciated — in some instances to a degree horrible to contemplate. They had no protection from the piercing night air, which could penetrate through the open sides of their cages, and strike into frames almost equally free from clothing and from flesh.

"While we had been making our tour of inspection the doomed culprit had been unlashed and dismounted from his horse at the gate. But when set on his feet he was unable to stand, owing to weakness and the constrained and painful position in which he had been kept so long, and his guard were obliged to carry him into the precincts of the prison. Here an ample breakfast had been provided, of which he ate heartily, and with evident enjoyment. After a full half hour it was intimated to him that his presence was expected. With the assistance of an attendant on each side, he walked slowly into the execution ground, and was placed, kneeling and sitting on his heels (in the universal Japanese posture), behind a small hole dug for the reception of his head. Some ten yards in front of him, and separated by a rope running across the square, sat the presiding yakonin and the prison authorities, calmly fanning themselves ; and beyond these again were the six or eight foreigners who had been admitted.

"The prisoner's arms were then pinioned behind his back; but, before the cloth was tied over his eyes he requested that a minute's grace might be allowed him. This being granted, he raised a weak, quavering voice to its highest pitch, and screamed out, "My friends !" Immediately an unearthly chorus of wails answered the poor wretch from his friends outside the walls, none of whom could be seen from the interior. This was followed by "Syonara" (good-bye), and by a deeper and more prolonged wail from the crowd outside. The prisoner then signaled to his guards that he was ready, and submitted quietly to the operation of blindfolding ; the executioner stepped up, and carefully adjusting the victim's head a little on one side, so as to hang exactly over the hole prepared to receive it, signified that all was ready; the word was given, when, without raising his weapon more than a foot above the neck of the condemned, the executioner brought down his heavy blade with an audible thud, which severed the head instantly from the body.

"Immediately the head fell it was seized, carefully washed and cleaned, the procession was reformed as before — except that the horse previously ridden by the deceased now carried the executioner in charge of the lifeless head — and wended its way to a raised mound at the side of the highway a quarter of a mile distant. Here a kind of gallows had been erected, and on this was placed the dead man's head, supported in its position by clay, there to remain for six days, in sight of all passers by, and a warning to all evil-doers."

(4.) *Blowing from cannon.*— Dr. Calkins[1] alludes briefly to this barbarous mode of putting to death which has been sometimes employed in quelling rebellions, in the following terms:

"The insurgent Sepoy, lashed to the cannon's mouth, within two seconds from the pulling of the trigger, is blown into 10,000 atoms." "Here," he adds, "is no interval for suffering, as no sooner has the peripheral sensation reached the central perceptive organ than that organ is dissipated on the four winds of heaven." Other allusions indicate that another form has prevailed; in which the living body of the offender is thrust into the cannon, forming, as one might say, a part of the charge. It is, however, needless for the duties of the commission to pursue descriptions in detail of barbarisms like these which cannot come under consideration in the present inquiry. The utmost that is even excusable is such brief mention of these monstrosities as may indicate the thoroughness of the research.

(5.) *Boiling.*— According to several authorities,[2] the death penalty has been, in earlier times, occasionally inflicted by boiling the offender, usually in hot water, sometimes in melted sulphur, lead or the like. The statute, 22 Henry VIII (1531), imposed this punishment, without

---

[1] Medico Legal Papers, 2d ser., 255.
[2] Leslie's Popular Monthly, March, 1886, page 343.

benefit of clergy, upon poisoners. It is said that the act was suggested by the crime of John Roose, cook to the Bishop of Rochester, who gave poison, mixed in porridge, to seventeen persons, ten of whom died; also, that Roose himself was the first sufferer, though this would be contrary to the modern rule which forbids *ex post facto* laws. The act was repealed not long afterwards, though not until several executions under it. The punishment of boiling in oil, says an ancient writer, is peculiarly appropriate in the case of women convicted of petit treason in attempting to poison their husbands. Nothing short of such a process could be relied on to permanently soften an individual so depraved.

(6.) *Breaking on the wheel.*— This mode of execution, although it has acquired some notoriety from the frequency with which it is mentioned in histories narrating the cruelties common in the middle ages, is really only a special form of beating to death. The condemned was lashed upon the periphery of a large wheel, which was caused slowly to revolve, and as it revolved he received a succession of blows from clubs in the hands of his executioners, or from bludgeons worked by clumsy machinery such as the times furnished; thus bruising the flesh, breaking the bones and steadily reducing the body to a mangled formless corpse. The "wheel"[1] was for centuries a common instrument of torture and death in several countries of Europe. It appears to have come first into use in Germany, where it was employed as early as the tenth century. Francis I., about 1525, introduced it into France. It was employed for a time also in England. The prisoner designed for death by this method was bound to an instrument rudely resembling a wheel, his legs and arms being separated as far as possible and attached to cross-bars corresponding to spokes. As the wheel revolved the limbs of the victim were fractured by blows from a heavy iron rod delivered below the knees and elbows. Sometimes the rod was held in position mechanically, the limbs of the prisoner, as he was whirled on the wheel, coming in contact with it. Usually, however, the rod was held in the hands of an executioner, who administered the blows as rapidly as he could wield it. In France the torture of this mode of punishment was lessened in many cases by heavy blows being dealt on the head and chest of the victim, so as to shorten life. These blows were called *coups de grace*, or strokes of mercy. (See Beating.)

---

[1] St. Louis Globe Democrat, November, 1877.

(7.) *Burning.*— It is familiarly known that one of the modes of inflicting death, frequently employed in early religious persecutions, was burning alive. To reproduce any of the soul-harrowing accounts of the tortures thus perpetrated in the name of religion is not necessary for our present purpose, the general facts, the stake to which the sufferer was lashed, the faggots which were around him piled, the blistering blaze, the suffocating smoke, the agonizing moments of protracted life, the speedy, none too speedy death, the removal of the half-burned body from the ashes, not yet cold, are well known to all readers of history. There may, however, be reason for mentioning that the use of burning has not been limited to religious discipline, so-called. Civil governments have employed it as a means of punishing crimes in the proper sense of the word. The Romans, the Jews and some other ancient nations are said to have inflicted it on betrayers of councils, incendiaries and persons guilty of incest. The ancient Britons punished heinous crimes by burning the offenders alive in wicker baskets. This form of death was used in colonial times in this country, for those who had been convicted of petty treason, one form of which was the murder of a master by his slave; and many persons are said to have been thus put to death in the various colonies from Massachusetts to Carolina.

A writer in a popular monthly [1] describes a peculiar mode of burning alive, or of rather roasting alive, which prevailed among the Chinese. It has been known as Pao-lo, and was invented by the Emperor Tcheon at the instigation of his favorite concubine Takya. The instrument for this punishment was a brass cylinder twenty cubits in height by eight in diameter, with openings at the bottom like a grate. Criminals had their arms and legs fastened around this cylinder, the fires were lighted within, and the unfortunate victims were roasted in this manner until they were reduced to ashes.

Another extraordinary method of the application of this punishment was that known as the *"illuminated body"* and was invented by Sefi II., Shah of Persia. [2] The victim was stretched upon a slab and fastened to it. Innumerable little holes were bored all over his body. These were filled with oil, a little taper was set in each hole and they were all lighted together. The poor victim perished in the most unspeakable agony.

---

[1] Frank Leslie, March, 1886, p. 343.
[2] Frank Leslie's Popular Monthly, March, 1886, p. 346.

A Gallic and British method of sacrificing criminals [1] is remarkable not only as indicating the sternness with which crime was repressed by a priesthood, but also from the resemblance which it bore to the punishment inflicted in England on traitoresses, as late as the eighteenth century. The offenders were thrown into cages of wicker-work, made in the form of some well known idol, and large enough to hold many human beings at once. Wood was heaped beneath and around them, and when all was ready the pile was kindled. The flames played about the fragile prison, and shot their forked tongues further and further into the mass of writhing and shrieking victims. The semblance of the god was soon lost to view, but not before the crowd around had, as it seemed, seen the god himself deal death to the wrong-doers in its most appaling form. Then came one great blaze of the pile and the cage and the wretches who had been within it, and when that died out justice was satisfied, and the gods were content for a time.

(8.) *Burying alive:*— This simple form has been employed among barbarous tribes and, in ancient times, even in civilized countries. The victim was not always completely interred. The allusions to the practice show that he was sometimes buried up to the hips or to the neck and shoulders, and then beaten or tortured to death or left to starve. In more civilized countries he was walled up in a cell.

(9.) *Crucifixion.*— No form of the death penalty has excited more attention and study, elicited a greater number of descriptions or aroused so deep and widespread horror and detestation than crucifixion. Dr. Lyman Abbott [2] gives the following account of the method especially as it was practiced in the case of our Savior:

" Of all the cruel punishments of a barbaric age, crucifixion was the most barbarous. It possessed a bad pre-eminence of cruelty in an age when fashionable audiences crowded the vast amphitheater to applaud the fearful horrors of gladiatorial combats, and fair women gave the death signal, and feasted their sanguinary eyes on the ebbing life of the defeated. It was in this age that Cicero called crucifixion a punishment most inhuman and shocking, and wrote of it that it should be removed from the eyes and ears and the thought of men. Too horrible for a Roman citizen, no freeman might be subjected to it. It was reserved, with rare exceptions, for slaves and

---

[1] Pike's History of Crime in England, vol. 1, p. 12.
[2] Dict. Rel. Knowledge, tit., Crucifixion.

foreigners. Upon this Gentile cruelty the Jew looked with especial horror. The cross, like the eagle, was a sign of degradation. Its infliction by the Romans was a badge of Israel's servitude. The ancient law of Moses affixed a peculiar curse to it. To crucify even a corpse was to submit it to the greatest possible indignity. Thus the agony of pain was intensified by the agony of a peculiar shame.

"The physical anguish of the cross was that of a lingering death. The victim's life was wrested from him in a fierce but predetermined battle that lasted always many hours, often several days. Every moment of this hopeless contest added new agony to an anguish at first almost unendurable. The form of the Latin cross is as familiar as it is sacred to all Christendom. The sufferer was usually bound upon it as it lay upon the ground. The hands and feet were then firmly nailed to the wood. Lest this fastening should prove too frail, a transverse piece of wood between the thighs afforded an additional support. The cross was then elevated, with the sufferer upon it, and fastened firmly in the ground. In this act the body was terribly wrenched. The concussion often dislocated the limbs. Then, hanging between heaven and earth, the victim was left to die. The hot rays of an Oriental sun beat down upon his naked body and unsheltered head. The ragged edges of his undressed wounds festered and inflamed. From these wounds shooting pains ran along in accelerating waves of increasing anguish. Every attempt to secure any relief from the unnaturally constrained position increased the torment. The blood, impeded in its circulation, flowed in slackened and laborious currents. An increasing fever consumed the body with internal fires; the head throbbed with anguish; the parched lips burned with a raging thirst. As death drew nigh insects swarmed upon the body, and birds of prey commenced to feast upon it before life was yet extinct. Yet no vital organ was directly touched, and the stubborn life surrendered to its invincible foe only after a long and protracted siege. Even the pittiless and stolid Roman endured not long the sight of sufferings at once so protracted and so intense. For death, if not hastened by other means, did not usually take place for four or five days. Rarely, however, was the criminal suffered to die by the mere infliction of the cross. A thrust with the spear or a blow with the club at length put an end to tortures which wearied even the patience of spectators. Crucifixion was not, however, uncommon in an age when no discrimination was made between punishment and revenge, and when ingenuity was exhausted in the endeavor to intensify the sufferings of those condemned for crime, or even captured in war. At the time of the siege of Jerusalem hundreds of Jews were crucified together, and left to hang in sight of the city walls."

From accounts given by other writers, which are very numerous, additional particulars may be gathered; some interesting as corroborating or explaining the brief narrative of our Savior's sufferings given by the Evangelists, others somewhat relevant to our present purpose, for they illustrate the different ways in which death on the cross was inflicted in various centuries and countries, a topic which the Evangelists had no occasion to consider.

Writers are not agreed as to the exact origin of the cross. Some attribute the invention of it to Semiramis; others hold that it may have been a gradual growth among barbarous tribes as a cruelty of war. Nearly all say that its use was very ancient, and very general among almost all communities but the Jews. There were several incidents introduced, some in one case, some in another, with a purpose of heightening the agony, of shortening the duty and care of the executioners, or perhaps of giving the victim the merciful relief of a speedy death. Previous to commencing the execution, the sufferer was scourged sometimes with the utmost severity. He was usually compelled to carry his own cross to the place appointed for the execution, commonly remote; and various tokens of the peculiar shame of the punishment were connected with this procession. Arrived at the fatal spot the sufferer was stripped nearly naked. He was fastened to the cross, then lying on the ground, either by spikes driven through his hands and feet, or, in another form of the punishment, by cords bound around them. There was a form of the punishment in which a tree or post was used; the hands being secured by one nail above the malefactor's head, while the feet were fastened by another nail below. The cross was then erected, its foot or base secured in the ground, and the sufferer left to await death by the slow increase of physical anguish. If the intensity of suffering was too slow in its effect for either the malice or the mercy of those in charge, the victim's legs were broken with heavy blows of a club, his vitals were pierced by thrusts of a spear, a fire was kindled around the foot of the cross, or wild beasts were admitted to gnaw his limbs. Some drugged drink was usually given. In one form the agony was aggravated by placing the criminal with the head downward. Great as was the suffering, such is the power of the human frame to bear it that there are narratives of cases in which life was prolonged many days, of others in which it lasted until starvation, not the torture of his situation, ended the victim's misery, of others in which a rescue even after a long time of exposure resulted in a recovery. It should be added that to prevent any interference, the custom was to keep guards stationed until death was assured. It is stated that crucifixion was abolished for Christian countries by the Emperor Constantine; and that at the present day the use of it is nearly confined to the Mahometans.

A punishment analogous to crucifixion was formerly practiced in the West India Islands.[1] The delinquent was suspended from a post by means of a hook inserted under his shoulder, or under his breastbone. In this manner he is prevented from doing anything to assist himself, and all persons are prohibited, under severe penalties, from relieving him. He remains in this situation, exposed to the scorching heat of the day, where the sun is almost vertical and the atmosphere almost without a cloud, and to the chilling dews of the night; his lacerated flesh attracts a multitude of insects which increase his torments, and under the fever produced by these complicated sufferings, joined to hunger and thirst, all raging in the most intense degree, till he gradually expires.

There was a peculiar punishment, and perhaps a capital one, called crucifrangium by the ancients, inflicted on Roman slaves and Christian martyrs, as also on women or girls. Under the reign of Diocletian twenty-three Christians suffered martyrdom in the same manner. The legs of the criminal were laid on an anvil and by main force fractured with a heavy hammer, somewhat similar to the more modern custom of breaking the bones of offenders on the wheel by an iron bar.

(10.) *Decimation.*— There have been instances of military crimes, such as mutiny, in which the number of offenders implicated has been so great that capital punishment of all has been deemed impracticable, both because it would involve a general indiscriminate slaughter too shocking to comtemplate, and because the military force involved could not bear the loss of so many men. A general in command cannot massacre an entire regiment on the eve of battle, no matter what the crime and the guilt of the regiment may have been. In such cases resort has been had to the expedient of marshalling the

---

[1] Jeremy Bentham, Rationale of Punishment, p. 168.

men lying under accusation by mere lot or chance and then ordering
the shooting of every tenth man. Evidently the form in which this
is done may be so varied that it shall be impossible that individuals
of the troop under condemnation shall know, until the fatal discharge
has occurred, to whom it will be fatal. The whole number are thus
kept under the terror of death, but a few only are sacrificed. There
is no opportunity to employ this expedient in civil government.

(11.) *Dichotomy.*— The word in its general use signifies cutting into
two parts; bisecting. Dr. Calkins[1] alludes to it as a mode of exercis-
ing the right of retaliation, and used as a method of capital punishment among primitive people, as enforced by the Prophet Samuel
upon Agag, king of the Amalekites, at Gilgal (I Sam. chap. xv), where
"Samuel hewed Agag in pieces before the Lord;" also as instanced in
the subjecting the Rabbites to saws and axes and a roasting in the
brick-kiln. Thus used the terms seem to include any rude, untaught
mode of fatally cutting the body asunder with an implement like a
sword; or, with a wooden saw, a martyrdom said to have been inflicted
upon the Prophet Isaiah, and to have been a not uncommon fate of
early Christians. Ep. Heb., chap. xi, says that "many were stoned,
were *sawn asunder.*" It is mentioned also[2] as a Babylonian custom;
but the passages in the Gospels will admit of the milder interpreta-
tion of scourging with severity, discarding from office, etc. Extended
particulars as to modes of punishment like these furnish no information instructive on the present inquiry.

(12.) *Dismemberment.*— There is no difficulty in believing that in
times and among people, where the chief effort in capital punishments
was to intensify agony and shame, the rude device of tearing the
body forcibly asunder would not pass unthought of. This element
entered into the punishment visited upon Ravaillac, who assassinated
Henry IV. of France, in 1610, which is noted as one of the most cruel
on record.[3] He was tied to a rack shaped like a St. Andrew's cross.
His right hand, within which was fastened the dagger by which he
killed the king, was thrust into a slow fire. Pincers then tore the
flesh from various parts of his body, and into the wounds they made,
boiling oil, lead, pitch and resin were poured. A horse was then
attached to each limb, and his joints were drawn asunder. Afterward

---

[1] Medico Legal Papers, 2d ser., p. 259.
[2] Kitto's Encyclopedia, vol. iii, p. 615.
[3] St. Louis Globe-Democrat, Nov., 1887; see for the text of the sentence,
Causes Celebres de Fouquier, 76 Livr.

the spectators dragged the body through the streets. So great was his power of will that he scarcely uttered a groan while these tortures were being inflicted; and he died without implicating any of his accomplices.

Obviously dismembering may naturally have been inflicted by employment of the crude machines which the dungeons of the period contained in great variety, as well as by fastening the limbs to horses and then starting the horses in opposite directions. But there is no need of pursuing the inquiry. The various accounts given justify us in saying that dismemberment is not to be regarded as a distinct mode of punishment, so much as an expression of atrocious cruelty sometimes attached to the death penalty.

Drawing and quartering was not a distinct punishment, but an adjunct or circumstance of aggravation formerly superadded in England, to hanging, in the more heinous crimes, particularly high treason. In the ancient and severer form, sentences involving drawing and quartering [1] directed that the offender should be drawn on a hurdle to the place of execution, and there hanged by the neck, but not until dead; that he should be taken down again, and while yet alive, his bowels should be taken out and burnt before his face; and that, afterwards, his head should be severed from the body, and the body divided into four quarters; and that his head and quarters should be at the king's disposal. The last clause was, in the severer forms of execution, carried into effect by an exposure in public, in conspicuous places; such as, the head at Temple Bar (if the execution took place in London), the four quarters at four of the gates of the city where the execution took place. This addition to hanging is said to have been introduced in England in 1241, during the reign of Henry III. Fosbrooke says (Encyc. Antiq.), that ancient gallows near London had hooks for eviscerating, quartering, etc., the bodies of criminals. A modified and more lenient form was introduced by statute 54 Geo. III., c. 146.

(13.) *Drowning.*— This simple primitive mode of punishment is often mentioned. It seems to have been in vogue in former days in Syria, Greece, Rome and Persia. The methods are described: One, that of attaching some heavy weight to the body, then casting into the sea or large river; the other that of sewing the living victim in a large bag or sack. It is said [2] that George, Duke of Clarence and

---

[1] Gabbett's Crim. Law, 503.   [2] 1 Howell's State Trials, p. 275.

brother to Edward IV. for bold and disorderly words of expostulation against an injustice done by the king, was committed close prisoner to the tower and there secretly put to death by immersing his head in a butt of Malmsey wine.

(14.) *Exposure to wild beasts, etc.*— Every one has been made familiar by such accounts as that of the Prophet Daniel, with the primitive practice of exposing criminals to be devoured by wild beasts. They were not always literally " cast into the den." The victim was shut into the cage where the wild beasts were kept confined; or, in some forms of the penalty, man and beast were ushered into the arena or the pit of the circus and allowed to contend as a public show or amusement.

A writer[1] says that death by the serpent's bite was a common form of administering capital punishment in the Oriental countries in ancient days, and it is said, the system has by no means become obsolete yet. Instances are on record in which offenders were bound naked in jungles in which vipers were numerous, and left to suffer a lingering and terrible death from the reptiles' fangs. Men and women and sometimes children, were thrown into caverns infested by venomous snakes to meet death in its most frightful form, in the darkness, among the bones of hundreds of persons whose lives had gone out in the same place and by the same means. Many British prisoners, it was told, were subjected to like treatment by the Sepoys during the mutiny about thirty years ago. Even at the present time, it is said, malefactors in some parts of India are thrown into large cages filled with serpents. Travelers in Persia tell stories about similar cruelties being inflicted on criminals in the wilder and more barbarous portions of that country.

By the ancient mode of executing parricides,[2] so heinous an offender was sewed in a sack alive, venomous serpents with him, and sometimes a dog, a monkey or the like were added. Vipers are mentioned in some accounts of similar executions.

In Cochin-China,[3] a woman convicted of adultery is trampled to death by an elephant, which is trained for that purpose; and in Tonquin,[4] female criminals are tied to a loose stake, and in that situation delivered to an elephant, who seizes them with his trunk, throws them into the air, then catches them on his tusks, and finishes by trampling them under his feet.

---

[1] St. Louis Globe Democrat, March, 1887. [2] 1 Pike, History of Crime, p. 15.
[3] 9 Pinkerton's Voyages and Travels, p. 770. [4] Page 758.

(15.) *Flaying alive.*— Stripping the skin from the body of the condemned while he yet lived was formerly used in England. It was, however, a barbarous mode of torturing an offender to death, rather than a punishment in a judicial sense.

(16.) *Flogging.*— *Knout.*— These modes of punishment, also covered by the terms "scourging," whipping have not been used, primarily, at least in European countries and in modern times as "capital punishments;" that is, have not been used where the sentence or judicial design has been to inflict death. But the punishment, even when death has not been the legal penalty, has often been fatal in its effects, either by reason of the intolerable number of the blows, or by the cruel severity with which they were given, or from the nature of the implement used, and doubtless flogging, in one or other of its forms, has often been imposed with the expectation and intent that it should result fatally. For this reason it may perhaps be mentioned in enumerating punishments styled "capital." Flogging with the "knout" has long been practiced in Russia, especially by the nobles in their manorial courts upon the serfs. Its method of infliction is as follows:[1]

The condemned man is conducted half naked to the place chosen for this kind of execution; all that he has on is a pair of simple linen drawers round his extremities; his hands are bound together, with the palms laid flat against each other; the cords are breaking his wrists, but no one pays the slightest attention to that. He is laid flat upon his belly, on a frame inclined diagonally, and at the extremities of which are fixed iron rings; his hands are fastened to one end of the frame, and his feet to the other; he is then stretched in such a manner that he cannot make a single movement, just as an eel's skin is stretched in order to dry. This stretching the victim causes his bones to crack, and dislocates them — what does that matter? The executioner advances a few steps with his body bent, holding the knout in both hands, while the long thong drags along the ground between his legs. On coming to about three or four paces from the prisoner, he raises, by a vigorous movement, the knout towards the top of his head, and then instantly draws it down with rapidity towards his knees. The thong flies and whistles through the air, and descending on the body of the victim, twines round it like a hoop of iron. In spite of his tension,

---

[1] Germain De Lagny, The Knout and the Russians, p. 179.

the poor wretch bounds as if he were submitted to the powerful grasp of galvanism. The executioner retraces his steps, and repeats the same operation as many times as there are blows to be inflicted. When the thong envelopes the body with its edges, the flesh and muscles are literally cut into strips as if with a razor, but when it falls flat, then the bones crack; the flesh in that case is not cut, but crushed and ground, and the blood spurts out in all directions. The sufferer becomes green and blue, like a body in a state of decomposition. The knout is fatal if the justice of the Czar or of the executioner desires it to be so.

(17.) *Garrote.*—This mode of execution seems to have been originally devised by the Moors and Arabs, and to have been taken from them by the Spaniards from whom it has been transmitted to the Spanish colonies in America.[1] In the earliest form it consisted in simply placing a cord round the neck of the criminal who was seated on a chair fixed to a post, and then twisting the cord by means of a stick inserted between it and the back of the neck till strangulation was produced. Afterward a brass collar was used, containing a screw which the executioner turned till its point entered the spinal marrow where that unites with the brain, causing instantaneous death.

It is said that in the days of the inquisition a strangulation by this method was granted as a mercy to heretics who recanted before executing on them the sentence of burning at the stake.

In Spain,[2] garroting takes place on a platform, during the day time and publicly, in the place destined in general for this purpose, or in that determined by the tribunal when especial causes render that necessary. The criminal is conducted to the scaffold in a black tunic (hopa) on horseback or in a cart, and the public crier publishes in a loud voice the sentence in the place of transit as ordered by the judge. If the criminal be a regicide or parricide the tunic is yellow, and he wears besides a cap (birreta) of the same color both covered with red spots. The body of the executed person remains exposed on the scaffold until one hour before sunset when it is buried. If his friends or relations beg the body for this purpose it is delivered to them, but the code prohibits the funeral being celebrated with pomp.

(18.) *Guillotine.*—This instrument of decapitation, which was brought into notoriety during the French revolution, received its

---

[1] People's Cyclopedia of Universal Knowledge, p. 779.

[2] Testimony taken by the British Commission, p. 516.

modern name from the person often called its inventor, Dr. Joseph Ignace Guillotin, of Lyons, in France, but who as writers of authority say was not strictly the inventor but the one who first urged and brought about its adoption as more humane than the ax and block, the gallows and like methods. It is thus described by a modern writer:[1]

"The essential parts of the guillotine are two upright posts mortised into one end of a platform and grooved on their inner face, the *couperet* or ax depending from a crossbeam above, and the *lunette* for steadying the head. The victim having been bound down in the prone position with head projecting, the ax thus far held in place by a ratchet-spring and now liberated, descends *au delic* with a force equal to the pressure of 12,800 kilogrammes (Du Camp), making the section near the root of the neck. The time required from the arrival of the cortege at the scaffold to the tumbling of the head into the pannier, is about six minutes. In 1793 twenty-one Girondists were dispatched in thirty-one minutes. Fouquier-Thienville made the boast that he, at a later date, had disposed of sixty-two of the same party in forty-five minutes."

A recent history of this machine,[2] says that an instrument of this kind was used in Germany early in the thirteenth century, and was known as the "Panke" or "Diele." In 1233 it was mentioned in the criminal statutes of the Netherlands, and its name appears in many accounts of executions in Germany and other countries about the same period. It was in active operation in Germany in the sixteenth century. Many such pictures are in existence, and in the old council chamber at Luneburg is preserved an ancient door, dating probably from the thirteenth century, on which is carved a representation of the guillotine in operation. In a work by Lucas Lossius, "Annotationes Scholasticae," printed at Frankfort in 1551, we find the picture of one of these instruments, which differs in several important points from the ordinary model. It consists of two short upright posts, with a block between them, on which rests the head of the kneeling victim. The blade is loosely fastened at the top of the posts, and is driven down upon the sufferer's neck by a sturdy blow from the executioner's heavy maul. Very similar to this instrument is one we find pictured in an engraving published in Frankfort by H. P. Rebenstock, in 1573, representing the execution of Manlius. Strange to say, the behead-

---

[1] Dr. Calkins, Medico Legal Papers, 2d Ser., p. 262.
[2] 45 Harper's Magazine, page 186.

ing of this old Roman by the guillotine was a favorite subject with the German artists of the sixteenth century. George Pens, a pupil of Albrecht Durer, engraved it on copper in 1553, as did likewise another pupil of the same master, Albrecht Aldegraver. From the inscription on the latter's work, it will be seen that it represents the execution of the younger Manlius. According to the custom of the time, when artists were not afraid of an anachronism, the Romans are depicted in the garb of the German knights of the sixteenth century. Here we see the guillotine of the French revolution, the ax suspended by a cord and running between grooved posts. Nothing is wanting but greater mechanical perfection in the gearing.

In Italy, a similar instrument, called the _mannaia_, was used for the execution of persons of quality. Beatrice Cenci suffered death by this instrument in 1599. In England a similar machine was used, and a full description of it may be found in the British State Calendar for 1708. The " maiden " of Scotland, which was used for the beheading of Morton in 1581, was an instrument similar to those already mentioned, and is supposed to have been brought over from Germany by the very man who suffered by it. It is still preserved in the museum of the Antiquarian Society at Edinburgh. Even France possessed it as early as the fifteenth century, under the name of " Doloire," and two centuries later the unfortunate Duke de Montmorency was executed with this instrument, at the instigation of Richelieu. It seems then to have passed out of use and to have been forgotten.

It was first tried on the 18th of April, 1792, upon a number of corpses at the Bicetre hospital, and was found to work with rapidity and precision. A week later it was employed for the decapitation of a convicted highway robber named Pelletier. The dreadful use to which it was afterward put in the wholesale massacre of innocent men, women, and even children, made its very name a horror, and probably contributed not a little to its not being adopted in England and the United States, instead of the gallows, as a means of inflicting capital punishment.

Dr. Guillotin himself narrowly escaped being a victim of the instrument which bears his name. He was thrown into prison during the reign of terror, but was released on the death of Robespierre, resumed the practice of his profession in Paris, and died quietly in his bed on the 26th of March, 1814. The story that he died brokenhearted because of the infamy attached to his invention is, of course, untrue.   Some additional information relative to the " Maiden " and other forerunners of the guillotine is[1] interesting.

The town of Halifax, in Yorkshire, having been anciently famous for the manufacture of woolen cloths, a law was made for the protection of the property of the manufacturers, by which it was ordained that persons convicted of stealing cloth from the tenter-grounds should be executed immediately after being convicted before two justices of the peace.   The machine by which persons thus convicted were executed, was constructed in the following manner: "Two strong wooden beams were fixed on a scaffold, and between them, in a transverse form, ran another beam, to the lower side of which was fixed a sharp instrument in the form of a chopping knife, with a large quantity of lead on the upper part.   The criminal put his neck between the two side beams, and the cross beam being drawn by a pulley, was suffered to fall down, and the head was severed from the body in a moment."   The Earl of Morton, regent in Scotland, returning from the Court of Queen Elizabeth, in the year 1574, saw this machine at Halifax, and had a model taken of it, with a view to the execution of such of the Scottish nobility as should 'oppose his measures; but it happened that his lordship was the first who suffered by this mode of execution; whence it was called the "Maiden."   After this many persons of rank in Scotland were executed by this machine; but Mr. Hamilton was the last who yielded his life in this manner; and the instrument of death is now kept in a room adjacent to the council chamber of Edinburgh.

(19.) *Hanging.*—The commission give at this point of the report a concise simple account of the process of execution by hanging in its physiological aspects, reserving the presentation of some special objections to the mode for a later place in this report.

As is well known, hanging is and has long been the mode of capital punishment employed in this State.   In its simplest form—that of suspending the criminal by a cord around his neck from a branch of a tree—it must have been of very early origin.   Accounts vary as to the date of the introduction of the gallows as the instrument. This seems to have occurred in Roman dominions soon after the Emperor Constantine abolished crucifixion.   An early form of this seems to have been a crude imitation of a tree—a tall post bearing at its top a projecting beam from the end of which the fatal cord

---

[1] 1 Jackson's Newgate Calendar, page 222

could be suspended. In the fifteenth century[1] a form was in use consisting of a beam balanced like the beam of a pair of scales, at the top of the post, from one end of which beam hung a halter, from the other end a large weight; and when the halter was pulled down and put around the offender's neck, the weight at the other end lifted him from the ground. A form very usual in England where the gallows or gibbet, as it is also called, was in use from about the middle of the fifteenth century, though there are historic allusions to its earlier use, consisted in two upright posts connected at the top by a cross beam from which the rope might be suspended. In employing the gallows the offender was, in early times driven to the place in a cart, which, after the rope was adjusted, was driven away from under the beam leaving the man to fall as far as the length of the rope permitted. In more recent times a similar fall is secured either by attaching a weight considerably heavier than the human body to the other end of the fatal rope, which passing through a wheel at the beam, pulls the body upward some feet when the weight is released; or by requiring the prisoner to stand while the rope is adjusted on a platform, the support of which is pulled away at the termination, when the body falls as far as the length of the rope permits.

Hanging has been for many years the characteristic mode of the death penalty for English dominions, so much so that a prominent writer[2] while conceding that as a legal mode of execution it is open to grave objections, yet expresses the deliberate opinion that "in England, whenever hanging is abolished capital punishment will be abolished also." In this country many animadversions have been bestowed upon it. Your commission believe that the following extract from a well known review[3] expresses correctly a feeling very common among the masses of our people, who, while they assent to capital punishment as a stern necessity, have not opportunity or means for forming an opinion on a preferable mode, and who are shocked by the frequent recurrence of this:

"A few weeks since three miserable men suffered the extreme penalty of the law in our Egyptian prison. After an impartial and careful trial they were found guilty, and were dealt with according to the prevailing human sense of justice. Yet such executions suggest most conflicting reflections even among those who strongly advocate capital punishment. We are led to wonder if the time will ever arrive

[1] Fosbrooke's Encyc. Antiq., 300.   [2] Pike, 2 History of Crime, 578.
[3] 52 Harper's Magazine, 462.

when the gallows shall be placed as a curiosity in museums, and sight-seers shall flock to gaze upon it and marvel how a people who gave evidence of so much civilization and refinement as did their forefathers (we shall be forefathers then) could have employed such a machine for the amelioration of the moral condition of mankind. Will posterity shudder at a model of a gallows set up in complete working order on a shelf, as we of to-day shudder when we examine the ancient instruments of torture collected in the Old World museums? Will the American of the year of our Lord 2,000 be so far in advance of us? We venture to hope so.

"In the meanwhile, since with our present lights we find nothing better to do with a murderer than to hang him, why may not merciful ingenuity devise some method of execution that shall not so very closely resemble the revolting act which the criminal expiates? It is, perhaps, a little significant that the gallows is the only piece of machinery that has stood stock-still in this era of progress. There it stands, the same clumsy, inefficient, inhuman thing it was when it first lifted its gastly framework into the air of the dark ages. If we must use it, let us see to it that it be adjusted with at least as much accuracy as an average apple-peeler."

The physiological aspect of hanging has been described[1] as follows:

"The immediate cause of death from hanging is suffocation, producing apoplexy. Other injuries are also sustained, e. g., pressure on the vessels and nerves, fracture of the spine or dislocation of the odontoid process. It was long supposed that apoplexy was the cause of death in hanging; but it is now ascertained that the pressure on the vessels of the neck only occasionally produces that sanguineous congestion in the brain which is remarked in apoplexy. An experiment made by Mr. Brodie renders it probable that the pressure sustained by the nerves would occasionally cause death or much inconvenience, allowing even the person to recover from the other consequences of hanging. It is now known that in hanging the circumstance that actually takes place, and which causes death, is a deep sleep, arising from the cerebral compression, unaccompanied with the symptoms that attend apoplexy, and in no case of recovery, followed by the ordinary termination of that disease, namely, paralysis. Fodera has collected some curious cases in illustration of this. Webfer mentions an instance of a man and a woman who survived hanging. The latter recollected nothing, and the former stated that on the appli-

---

cation of the cord he felt no pain, but sunk, as it were, into a profound sleep. Morgagni also mentions that an individual, who recovered under similar circumstances, informed him that the first sensation was flashes of light from his eyes, and that he then sunk into the same sleep. Another case is related on the authority of Lord Chancellor Bacon. A gentleman took a fancy to ascertain whether those who were hung experienced any pain, and actually performed the experiment on himself. He immediately lost all consciousness, and the event would have terminated tragically had a friend not entered in time to cut him down. Hence it seems most probable that asphyxia precedes death, which however, will certainly follow, if timely aid be not afforded. The second cause of death from hanging is one from which there is no relief. It consists, in addition to the compression, of a laceration of the trachea or larynx, or a luxation or fracture of the cervical vertebræ, occasioned by a rupture of the ligaments of the neck. The celebrated Louis inquired of several executioners how they saved the lives of some criminals while others were irrecoverably dead? They answered that they caused, in the latter case, a laceration of the trachea, and luxation of the first cervical vertebræ from the second, by placing the knot of the cord under the neck and then giving a rotatory motion to the body at the moment when the ladder was taken from his feet. This luxation chiefly occurs in heavy persons, or where they may have fallen from a height upon the end of the rope, or where attempts have been made to hasten death by increasing the weight of the body. So violent, also, is this sort of death, that the fæces, urine, and even the semen, are often expelled. And the rapidity of the extinction of life is well illustrated by the result, in cases where the vertebræ are injured. Similar questions to those which arise on viewing the body of a person found dead in the water present themselves when a body is found suspended.

A learned physician thus contributes the following careful scientific observations on the subject:[1]

" The body precipitated and abandoned, there is usually an interval of immobility, lasting perhaps a minute (save in the swinging around once or twice from the tendency of the cord to untwist itself upon a strain); brilliant flashes then flit before the eyes, and ringing sounds not unlike oppressive music fill the ears, the legs feel an unwonted heaviness and drag, the face becomes phlogosed from constriction

---

[1] Med. Legal Papers, 2d ser., pp. 266–268 and 271.

upon the external jugulars, and the tongue, also congested, often protrudes. The brain itself may be anaemic. Consciousness, variable in continuance, may be early interrupted (Tardieu), and convulsions or throes, moderate or intense (though automatic only after the repression of sense), are present in the majority."

The Cord.— The progress of strangulation is regulated much by the position and action of the *cord.* If there is free play through the spiral knot, an equable pressure is established all around, and but that the internal jugulars, as being more deep seated, are less liable to compression than the carotids, a blood stasis might be established. The *Clove-Hitch,* as adverted to on the Avery-Cornell trial, is unadapted to the exigency. Laceration of the trachea is very rare. Dr. Plot, who figured somewhat in the reign of Henry VI, describes an escape through an ossification of the part. The popular notion that constriction is most thorough when the knot is disposed *under the ear,* (i. e., over the carotid of that side), is a misconception. Bring the knot to the sulcus above the pomum Adami, it makes a *point d' appui* in front, having for its *piece de resistance* or fulcrum the rigid vertebral column aback. With this arrangement a short fall suffices, as appears from records kept at the Mazas prison in France. Of 261 deaths from suicide effected here prior to 1870, most of the bodies, when discovered, were found touching by the toes or else resting upon the knees, a few were asquat some had a foot raised upon a chair. The explanation is this: Out of 143 cases specified, 117 had the knot in the sulcus, twenty-three opposite the laryngeal box, and three only over trachea below, but below the ear not one. Burke, the dissecting-room caterer, had a way of seizing the throat by a grip from behind; the thumbs, one over the other, being pressed into this same sulcus. There is another idea afloat, that a *bull-neck* makes a slow death. Doubtless the *vis inertiæ* or sag of an athletic frame may scarcely in many instances overbalance the physical resilience of the subject, and, of consequence, violent struggles may supervene. Gibbs, hanged at Bedloe's Island, 1831, suffered mightily, as did Payne, one of the four Lincoln plotters. The negro, Hanky Jones, now beyond the natural span of life, and so of reduced animal stamina, with the further advantage of a ten-foot fall, nevertheless, likewise suffered as acutely, or yet more so.

Surviving sensations. — What is the precise quality and what the degree of intensity of the suffering during the agony, is conjectural only in part. Fleischmann, in his own case, remarked, that following the slight uneasiness which was due to the tightening of the cord there was no conscious uneasiness. A woman (Faûre), resuscitated after a suspension of seven minutes, lost all sense whatever the instant after launching off. Montaignac, saved at the intercession of Turenne (the cord having snapped), declared that all pain vanished in a moment, and that in the acme of the paroxysm, a vivid light pervaded his entire body, conveying a transcendent charm. (Congestion of the brain was the proximate cause here.) Provided syncope be pre-established, any recurring convulsionary struggles may be mere reflex movements.

The same learned physician furnishes the following (id., p. 271) abstract of sixty-five recent cases, comprised between 1869 and 1873: Average time in 49, 11:15 minutes. Cord — right or maladjusted, 5; deficient in length, 3; in excess, 1; ruptured, 8; repeated rupture, 1.

Throes and contortions — Severe and continuous, 23; moderate, 14; feeble and evanescent, 18; chest heavings (indicative of persisting sensation), 8.

Fracture or luxation — Evident, 6; partial, 4; doubtful, 7; by the New York method, none.

Fall in feet — Average in four of the six cases, $7\frac{3}{4}$.

(20.) *Hari kari* (translated "happy dispatch," and otherwise called hari kiru or haro wo kiru, " belly cut "), is a curious punishment attributed to Japan. It consists in the condemned man's disemboweling himself by ripping his abdomen open by sword thrusts, first upwards then again across. According to one class of accounts, this is done in obedience to a judicial sentence. According to others, the criminal is not strictly sentenced to be his own executioner, but pending proceedings against him he is allowed to commit suicide in the manner above described, with the legal effect that although he loses his life, which he would probably have done in any event, he evades trial, and secures to his family his property, which otherwise would have been forfeited to the State. The *hari kari* is said to be practiced in the case of officials strongly suspected of dishonorable crimes connected with administration of government.[1]

(21.) *Impalement.*— This consisted in crushing the body downward upon the point of a spear fixed in the ground, point upward, upon the point of sharpened pike or post, or the like, and leaving him there to die. It was a crude species of crucifixion.

In a history of Siam,[2] the following peculiar method of impalement

---

[1] Johnson's New Universal Cyclopedia, vol. II, title Hari kari; 28 Harper's Magazine, 182; 12 Harper's Magazine, 460.

[2] Vol. 9, Pinkerton's Voyages and Travels, page 594.

is described as the legal mode of punishing assassins. The criminal is made to lie down on his belly, and after being securely tied, a stake of wood is forced up his fundament by the blows of a club, and it is driven till it comes out, either through the stomach or through the shoulders ; they afterwards raise this stake and stick it in the earth.

(22.) *Iron Maiden.*—A machine for beheading, called "maiden," is mentioned under the title guillotine. There was a contrivance for causing death by sheer compression, known in the books as the "Scavenger's Daughter," which is somewhat described under pressing to death. Allusions in some accounts of martyrdoms, under the Inquisition, indicate that a machine was employed, consisting of an image or statue of the Virgin, which was so equipped with secret springs that when a suspected heretic endeavored to obey the command that he should kiss the Virgin, a multitude of concealed knives sprang forth and stabbed him. It is uncertain whether such allusions refer to any instrument of punishment employed by the civil courts, or to some contrivance for torture.

(23.) *Peine Forte et Dure.*—This consisted in superimposing a heavy weight upon the chest, that should suffice to reduce the breathing to a gradual minimum. It was not strictly a capital punishment, but a means of compelling the accused, if recusant, to plead to the indictment.

A learned writer[1] thus describes it : Before the infliction of this "*peine forte et dure,*" the acused was warned three times of the penalty which would attend obstinate silence, and allowed a few hours for consideration. If the prisoner, whether man or woman, still persisted, there was pronounced the judgment of penance ; that you be taken back to the prison whence you came, to a low dungeon into which no light can enter ; that you be laid on your back on the bare floor, with a cloth round your loins, but elsewhere naked ; that there be set upon your body a weight of iron as great as you can bear, and greater ; that you have no sustenance save, on the first day, three morsels of the coarsest bread, on the second day three draughts of stagnant water from the pool nearest the prison door ; on the third day, again three morsels of bread as before, and such bread and such water alternately from day to day until you die. This horrible suffering[2] was inflicted upon mutes, or those who refused to plead

---

[1] Pike, History of Crime, vol. 1, p. 387.

[2] Frank Leslie's Popular Monthly, March, 1886, p. 346.

"guilty" or "not guilty," when arraigned for treason or felony, or who made answers foreign to the purpose. By 12 George III., 1772, judgment was awarded against mutes as if they were convicted or had confessed. ·A man refusing to plead was condemned and executed at the Old Bailey, on a charge of murder, 1778, and another, on charge of burglary, at Wells, 1792. Walter Caverly, of Caverly, in Yorkville, England, having murdered two of his chidren and stabbed his wife, in a fit of jealousy, being arraigned for his crime at the York assizes, stood mute, and was thereupon pressed to death in the castle, a large iron weight being placed upon his breast, August 5, 1605. Major Strangeway suffered death in a similar manner at Newgate, in 1657, for the murder of his brother-in-law. Margaret Clitheroe, charged with harboring a priest, died under the horrible *peine forte et dure*. An act was, however passed in 1827, by which the court was directed to "enter a plea of 'not guilty' when the prisoner will not plead." The only case in this country was that of Corey, pressed to death in Massachusetts during the witchcraft delusion.

(24.) *Poisoning.*— It was early obvious that death sentences might be very conveniently executed by administering some poisonous drug, and the oft published narrative of the death of Socrates has made this mode familiar. No extended discussion of it would be useful.

(25.) *Pounding in mortar.*— Kitto seems to be of opinion[1] that the familiar verse (Prov. 27, 22) alludes to some such method of punishment.

(26.) *Precipitation.*—Casting offenders from some lofty precipice or building is a mode of execution very ancient. The "Tarpeian Rock," a mountainous projection on one side of the Capitoline Hill in Rome, was often resorted to by the Romans for this species of punishment, which acquired the name of casting from the Tarpeian Rock. Amariah, king of Judah, is said to have sacrificed 10,000 Idumean captives by compelling them to leap from the summit of a precipice.

(27.) *Pressing to death.*— This was the principle embodied in the *peine forte et dure*, already described. There have been some other modes of using it. The Romans are said to have employed, occasionally, a punishment in which the condemned was laid under a hurdle and crushed by a weight of stones thrown upon it. In a machine called the Scavenger's Daughter[2] death was caused by an ingenious process of compression. The legs were forced back to the thighs, the thighs were pressed on to the belly, and the whole

---

[1] 3 Encyclopedia, p. 615. [2] 2 Pike, History of Crime, 87.

body was placed within two iron bands, which the torturers drew
together with all their strength until the miserable human being lost
all form but that of a globe. Blood was forced out of the tips of the
fingers and toes, the nostrils and the mouth, and the ribs and breast
bone were commonly broken in by the pressure. And a recent
writer[1] relates that in the citadel of an Indian prince was found the
instrument by which he put criminals to death. It consisted of two
large plates of iron, one lying flat on the ground, the other of great
weight, suspended in the air. The culprit was laid on the lower plate,
then the ropes holding the other were cut, and down it came, smash-
out the body as flat as a pancake. Finally it was taken out and
dried in the sun to be exhibited ever after as a terror to malefactors·

(28.) *Rack.*—This seems to have been chiefly used as an instrument
of torture of the living, though often fatal in its effects. The sufferer
was bound to a low structure having the shape of a bedstead, his
hands being lashed to a species of windlass at the upper end, his feet
to another windlass at the lower end. By turning these windlasses
ever so slightly, but with gradual, steady increase, the intensest
suffering could be inflicted. The prisoner seemed[2] in danger of
having the fingers torn from the hands, the toes from the feet, the
hands from the arm, the feet from the legs, the forearms from the
upper arms, the legs from the thighs and the thighs and the upper
arms from the trunk. Every ligament was strained, every joint
loosened in its socket; and if the sufferer remained obstinate when
released, he was brought back to undergo the same cruelties, with
the added horror of past experience and with diminished fortitude
and physical power.

(29.) *Running the gauntlet.*—This phrase denotes a method used in
some armies, where the condemned is compelled to run between two
lengthy parallel lines of soldiers, each of whom is charged with the
duty of giving him a blow with a rod, scourge or whip. The Russian
mode is thus described in an account which is abridged:[3]

At a given signal the sufferer has to advance with a slow step
between rows of soldiers, each of whom in turn must apply a vigorous blow on his back; the pain he endures might perhaps suggest
the idea of passing as quickly as possible through the double row of

---

[1] Dymond, The Law on its Trial, p. 290.
[2] 2 Pike, History of Crime, p. 87.
[3] De Lagny's Knout and Russians, p. 182.

executioners, in order to lessen the number and force of the blows which hack his flesh to pieces; but the officers drag the unhappy wretch forward or push him back. Every one must do his duty. The sufferer advanced up to the nine hundreth and third stroke; he did not utter a single cry or prefer a single complaint; the only thing which betrayed his agony, from time to time, was a convulsive shudder. The foam then began to form upon his lips and the blood to start from his nose. After fourteen hundred strokes his face, which had long before begun to turn blue, assumed a greenish hue, his eyes became haggard and almost started out of their sockets, from which large blood-colored tears trickled down and stained his cheeks. He was gasping and gradually sinking. The officer who accompanied me ordered the ranks to open and I approached the body. The skin was literally ploughed up, and had, so to say, disappeared. The flesh was hacked to pieces and almost reduced to a state of jelly; long strips hung down the prisoner's sides like so many thongs, while other pieces remained fastened and glued to the sticks of the executioners. The muscles, too, were torn to shreds. No mortal tongue can ever convey a just idea of the sight. The commandant caused the cart which had brought the prisoner to be driven up. He was laid in it on his stomach, and although he was completely insensible, the punishment was continued upon the corpse until the surgeon appointed by the government, who had followed the execution step by step, gave orders for it to be suspended. He did not do this, however, until there was hardly the slightest breath of life left in the sufferer's body. When the execution was stopped, 2,619 strokes had cut the body to pieces.

(30.) *Shooting.*—This has become, very naturally, a mode of executing death sentences of courts-martial in the armies of civilized nations. Capital punishment, says Simmons,[1] may be either by shooting or hanging. For mutiny, desertion, or other military crime, it is commonly by shooting, for murder not combined with mutiny, for treason and piracy, accompanied with murder or attempt to murder, by hanging.

Winthrop, a leading authority on the subject in the United States, says:[2] "Our Code does not prescribe in any case what form of death

---

[1] Courts-martial (5 ed.), sec. 645; also Griffith Military Laws, 86, quoted in the opinion of the U. S. Supreme Court in Wilkeson v. Utah, 99 U. S., 130.

[2] Military Law, 590.

penalty shall be imposed. It would, therefore, be strictly legal for a court-martial to sentence simply that the offender be punished "with death," the authority empowered to approve the sentence thereupon directing as to the mode — shooting or hanging — which the usage of the service, in the absence of statutory requirement, has designated as appropriate to the particular offense. In practice, however, the court invariably specifies the form of the penalty, adjudging in general that the accused be shot when convicted of desertion, mutiny, or other purely military offense, and that he be hung where convicted of a crime other than military, as murder, rape, or the crime of a spy."

He continues, describing the manner of a military execution:

"The reviewing authority, on approving the sentence, will designate such time and place as the convenience or interests of the service may dictate. Where, on account of some exigency, it is found impracticable to proceed with the execution at the time named or at the place selected, another time or place may at the earliest opportunity be indicated, and the execution legally proceed according to the new designation. By the same authority, an inferior commander — as the officer in command of the post or of the regiment, brigade, etc., at which the prisoner is held or to which he belongs — may be, and usually is, ministerially charged with the direction of the act of execution.

"In the absence of an army regulation prescribing a ceremonial for the execution of a capital sentence, the form may be varied in its details at the discretion of the commander, as the want of proper facilities or the exigences of the service may require, and in time of war the procedure is often materially simplified. According to the general usage, where the death penalty is to be inflicted by shooting, the prisoner, accompanied by the chaplain, is conducted by a detachment, including a firing party and coffin bearers, and headed by the provost-marshal or other officer and band playing the dead march, to an open space on three sides of which the command is formed facing inwards. The prisoner being placed, the charge, finding, sentence and orders are read aloud. The firing is directed by the officer, and the execution being completed, the command breaks into column and marches past the body."

The Commission are informed that in military shooting, the custom prevails of loading a portion of the muskets to be used by the firing party with ball cartridge and the remainder with blank. The pieces are then drawn at random by the soldiers, each of whom is by that means kept ignorant whether he or some other inflicts the fatal wound.

(31.) *Stabbing.*—Some ingenious modes have been invented for intensifying and prolonging death by stab wounds. There is a familiar story of a unique punishment inflicted on the Roman General Regulus by the Carthagenians. After capturing him in war they despatched him to Rome to bring about a treaty of peace. Rome declined, on the advice of Regulus, to enter into such a compact, and he returned to the Carthagenian camp, although he knew the failure to secure the treaty would mean death to him if he came within the power of that people. He was executed, so the legend says, by being thrown in a barrel studded with spear heads and rolled down hill.

A writer[1] says that among the military punishments inflicted during the fifteenth and sixteenth centuries in France and Germany, was the one known as *Passer par les Armes.* The accused was tried by forty of his peers, and if the verdict was not agreeable to the people, the case was submitted to another forty, and even to a third, until a satisfactory decision was reached. If adverse to the prisoner, he was executed then and there. A circle of spearsmen was formed around him, and amid the beating of drums, the circle narrowed around the victim until his body was transfixed with lances.

Figuier[2] says that in one of the modes the victim was securely tied to a post, his feet and hands fastened with ropes, his head is placed in a kind of pillory, while the magistrate delegated to witness the execution of the sentence, draws from a covered basket a knife, on the handle of which is written the part of the body in which it is to be inserted. This horrible torture is continued until chance selects the heart, or some other vital part. Generlly, the convict's friends purchase the connivance of the magistrate, who takes care to draw at the first venture, the knife intended for the mortal blow.

(32.) *Stoning* — Sometimes called "Lapidation," is so often mentioned in the Old Testament that its general nature is perfectly familiar. The Israelites probably brought the method from Egypt. As it was administered under the direction of Moses, the first stone was cast by the witnesses, two of which were required by the Mosaic law to obtain a conviction. If the first blows were not fatal, as easily they might be made to be, other stones were cast by bystanders. The placing the responsibility of commencing the execution on the witnesses is believed to have been a safeguard against perjury, as persons testi-

[1] Leslie's Monthly Magazine. [2] The Human Race, p. 294.

fying to a capital crime knew that they did so under a probability that they would be required to take a prominent part in the execution.

Kitto remarks[1] that stoning was probably the only punishment ordered by Moses; also that neither this nor any other punishment, according to his law, was attended by insult or torture; nor did such laws admit of the horrible mutilations practiced by other nations.

(33.) *Strangling.*— The descriptions of executions by hanging (already given), can be said of that punishment as a method of strangling. Other methods, however, have been in use. Among the Chinese[2] strangulation is effected by means of a silken cord that two executioners pull at each end, or by an iron collar tightened by a screw, very much like the garrote at present used in Spain. Strangulation by the silken cord is reserved for the princes of the imperial family; the collar is used to destroy, in the silence of the prison, those whose death it is desired to conceal.

Another writer[3] gives the following account: Criminals are sometimes strangled with a bow-string, but on general occasions a cord is made use of, which fastens the person to a cross, and one turn being taken around his neck, it is drawn tight by an athletic executioner. Men of distinction are usually strangled as the more honorable death; and where the emperor is inclined to show an extraordinary mark of attention toward a mandarin condemned to die, he sends him a silken cord, with permission to be his own executioner.

One antique mode of strangling[4] was by immersing the convict in clay or mud, and then strangling him by a cloth twisted around his neck.

The following account of an execution by strangling by the cord, which took place in Portugal,[5] further illustrates the subject:

"At eight o'clock the mournful procession was formed at the prison of the Lemoira, about a mile from the place of execution; the seven unhappy men, with fourteen priests, one on each side of each prisoner, in the center; the prisoners bare-footed and bare-headed, dressed in long white habits, with a hood hanging down behind, each bearing a small wooden crucifix in his clasped hands, secured together by bilts at the wrists. They were strongly guarded, both before and behind At each church they had to pass the procession stopped to hear an

[1] Ency., vol. 3, p. 615.
[2] Figuer, "The Human Race," p. 294.
[3] The Punishments of China, Lond., 1801.
[4] Smith's Bible Dic., tit. Punishments.
[5] Spear on Capital Punishment, 11th ed., 1845.

exhortation, so that it was near twelve o'clock before they reached the fatal place. One at a time ascended the platform, up a broad flight of steps, accompanied by two priests, as in the procession, and was immediately placed on the seat, with his back to the upright post. The hangman, a miserable wretch, walking with a crutch, then secured the legs, the arms and body of the unhappy man with cords, and placing a short cord round his neck and round the post, he put the hood over the face, and then, going behind the post, introduced a short, thick stick, and, giving it four or five turns, produced strangulation. The body was then untied and laid at a convenient distance, and another brought up from the foot of the scaffold, until the whole had suffered. The youngest, or least criminal, was executed first, and as each occupied fifteen or twenty minutes, the last had to endure, for at least two hours, the horrid sight of the sufferings of his fellow-prisoners. The mind can scarcely imagine a more dreadful state of mental suffering. When the whole were strangled the hangman wiped his face, and, seating himself in the fatal seat, coolly smoked a cigar, regaled himself with a bottle of wine, and then placing a block of wood under the neck, proceeded to cut off the heads, from which the blood flowed copiously in streams from the platform; then collecting the cords, and coolly wiping the hatchet and knife in one of the white dresses, he left the platform, first throwing the heads and bodies in a heap over the iron gate below. The fire was kindled, and in a few moments the whole was in a blaze. By six o'clock the whole was burnt to ashes, when a gang of galley-slaves, with irons on their legs, took the ashes in handbarrows and threw them into the Tagus."

In the land of the Ottoman, the bow-string is the favorite resort.[1] The condemned being seated upon a divan, two stout dwarf-mutes — misshapen figures — monsters, deaf and dumb — bend to an extreme a stout bow, and so making a loop of the cord, dexterously throw it over the head to encircle the neck. Life goes with a few brief struggles.

Bentham[2] thinks that while strangling by the bow-string may to some, perhaps, appear a severer mode of execution than hanging, partly from the prejudice against every usage of despotic governments, partly to the greater activity exerted by executioners in this case than in the other, yet the fact is, that it is much less painful than the other, for it is much more expeditious. By this means the force is applied directly in the direction which it must take to effect the obstruction

---

[1] Dr. Calkin's Medico-Legal Papers, 2d ser., 268.
[2] Rationale of Punishments, 108.

required; in the other case, the force is applied only obliquely, because the force of two men pulling in that manner is greater than the weight of one man. It is not long, however, in hanging, before a stop is put to sense; as is well enough known from the accounts of many persons who have survived the operation. This, probably, is the case a good while before the convulsive strugglings are at an end, so that in appearance the patient suffers more than he does in reality.

(34.) *Suffocation.* — Several writers say that this means of producing death has been employed as punishment. Thus, among the Persians, for great criminals a high tower was filled a great way up with ashes, the criminal was thrown into it, and the ashes, by means of a wheel, were continually stirred up and raised about him until he was suffocated. The story that the two English princes, children of Edward IV, confined in the tower by the hunchback, were smothered between bed-pillows, is familiar. According to Tacitus, the Rhenish tribes buried adulteresses in peat bogs. It is related that, in Algiers. Marshal Pelissier once smoked to death a native force that had retreated to a stronghold, a cave of rocks, and that a Roman emperor once commanded that an offender should be suffocated with the smoke of green wood, a crier proclaiming, "Let him who has sold smoke, suffer by smoke." [1]

PRESENT METHODS OF EXECUTION IN CIVILIZED COUNTRIES.

The present mode of execution in the various countries and the method of their application, were very carefully considered in the shape of answers to a series of printed questions, issued by the Capital Punishment Commission and presented to the Houses of Parliament in England in 1866. That commission was appointed to inquire into the provisions and operation of the laws under which the punishment of death was then inflicted in the United Kingdom, the manner of infliction, and to report whether it was desireable to make any alteration therein. The report practically advocates the abolition of capital punishment in a great many cases, but was a divided report in that respect, and therefore is only incidentally of value in connection with the subject entrusted to your commission. The answers, however, to these questions (which are tabulated as follows) show that, in substance, executions at the present day are either by the guillotine, as in France, Bavaria, Hanover, Belgium and Saxony; by

---

[1] III Kitto's Encyclopedia, p. 615; VIII McClintock and Strong's Encyclopedia.

48   [SENATE,

the garrote, as in Spain; by decapitation or hanging as in Russia; by
strangulation or decapitation, as in China; by beheading, as in
Switzerland and Denmark; by shooting as in the ordinary cases of
military law, and in some portions of Germany and South America;
by decapitation as in Prussia, and in other countries, and particularly
in the United States, universally by hanging, that being the old
common law method of execution inherited by the colonies from the
mother country, Great Britain, and still there existing.

Country.	Method.	Publicity.
Austria	Gallows	Public.
Bavaria	Guillotine	Private.
Belgium	Guillotine	Public.
Brunswick	Axe	Private.
China	Sword or cord	Public.
Denmark	Guillotine	Public.
Ecuador	Musket	Public.
France	Guillotine	Public.
Hanover	Guillotine	Private
Holland	Gallows	Public.
Italy	Sword or gallows (abolished)	Public.
Oldenberg	Musket	Public.
Portugal	Gallows	Public.
Prussia	Sword	Private.
Russia	Musket, gallows or sword	Public.
Saxony	Guillotine	Private.
Spain	Garrote	Public.
Switzerland :		
Fifteeen cantons	Sword	Public.
Two cantons	Guillotine	Public.
Two cantons	Guillotine	Private.

SUMMARY.

Guillotine 10   Musket 2   Public.... 29
Sword 19   Axe 1   Private ... 7
Gallows 3   Cord 1

Second. A careful review of the foregoing discloses these facts:
(1.) That the effort to diminish the increase of crime by the indiscriminate application of capital punishment to various offenses,
involving different grades of moral turpitude ; or, in other words, by

the enlarging of the number of offenses to which capital punishment
is made applicable, has proved a failure.

(2.) That any undue or peculiar severity in the mode of inflicting
the death penalty neither operates to lessen the occurrence of the
offense, nor to produce a deterrent effect.

(3.) That from the long catalogue of various methods of punishment adopted by various nations at different times, only *five* are now
practically resorted to by the civilized world.

These various existing modes will next be separately considered,
as a review of the objections attending them is directly within the
province of this commission, and, in the opinion of its members, furnishes very cogent reasons why the conclusions to which they have
arrived and the recommendations which they make should receive
earnest attention.

OBJECTIONS TO EXISTING MODES OF EXECUTION.

1. *The guillotine.*— A prominent, and, as your commission think,
a sufficient objection to the use of the guillotine, is the profuse effu-
sion of blood which it involves. It is, above all others, essentially a
bloody method. This feature, even if the execution is strictly private, must be needlessly shocking to the necessary witnesses, and
when the public are permitted to see the details the injury to humane
feelings is unquestionable and unbalanced by any compensating
advantage. Says a writer,[1] after describing an execution in recent
times of three men by the guillotine :

" The guillotine is apparently the most merciful, but certainly the
most terrible to witness, of any form of execution in civilized Europe.
The fatal chop, the raw neck, the spouting blood, are very shocking
to the feelings, and demoralizing, as such exhibitions cannot fail to
generate a love of bloodshed among those who witness them."

Your commission have not failed to observe that several writers,
whose opinions are deserving of the highest respect, have considered
the adoption of the guillotine as a substitute for hanging worthy of
consideration ; and so it is, for in the final issue it is instantaneous,
and, therefore, painless, and it is certain, that is, beyond all possibility
of resucitation. Doubtless the evil effects of it, as a scene, could be
greatly diminished by insuring a strict privacy. But the general
effect of the idea that such a sentence had been passed, and was to
be or had just been carried into effect, as that idea would inevitably

---

[1] Harper's Magazine, vol. 3, p. 78.

be presented to the public in the journals of the week and in general conversation, associated as it is with the bloody scenes of the French Revolution, would be found totally repugnant to American ideas. The plan of substituting the guillotine, or, indeed, any form of decapitation, has been wholly and unhesitatingly rejected.

2. *The garrote.*— This method presents the advantages of celerity and certainty, in both which hanging is deficient ; but it is scarcely less distressing when presented distinctly to the imagination, than is the guillotine. Physiologically considered, it involves two causes of death, one a mashing of the spinal column, the chief bone of the body ; the other a strangulation analagous to that produced in hanging. No reasons are seen why two fatal elements should be employed. Surely an apparatus can be arranged such that one, single, simple cause of death can be put in operation quickly, certainly and humanely. To multiply the causes savors of barbarity. It is true that the profuse exhibition of blood, so objectionable in the use of the guillotine, is not involved in employing the garrote; but medical men say that the fatal screw cannot be depended upon to be so quick and certain in operation that there may not be great agony on the part of the subject. Dr. Calkins[1] says that Lopez, the filibuster, executed by the garrote, at Havana, 1857, "had a speedy as well as an easy death." But that this is the universal or even the general rule is not established. Moreover, the garrote has been chosen as the means of judicial death in one only of the civilized jurisdictions, Spain and her colonies. They have employed it for more than a century, yet it has not been improved, nor has it been adopted by any other nation whose decision might be deemed an instructive example. In the opinion of your commission it is not desirable as a substitute for the method heretofore used in this State.

3. *Shooting.*— This mode has practically become confined to military executions, for which it is perfectly well adapted, for the reasons, among others, that the means needful are always at hand, and competent executioners are in readiness. If used in civil life, it would be bloody in its character and effects, would lack the celerity and certainty which are important (as is shown by the closing sentence of the official directions for a British execution — if the prisoner be not killed the provost-marshal goes up and shoots the prisoner through the head) would be objectionable as requiring the attendance of a

---

[1] Med. Legal Papers, 2d ser., pp. 270, 271.

number of executioners, and, further, demoralizing particularly
because of its tendency to encourage the untaught populace to think
lightly of the fatal use of fire-arms. In countries where a military
despotism was the prevailing form of government, such a mode of
executing the convictions of civil courts may have been tolerated; but
its employment in civil life in this country, would not tend, in the
judgment of your commission, to promote the orderly administration
of justice.

OBJECTIONS TO THE EXISTING METHODS OF HANGING.

4. Your commission next present the principal objections to the
present method of execution by *hanging*. And, first, as to the demoralizing effect of giving stimulants to the condemned immediately
before execution.

That a practice prevails of indulging condemned men in liquor,
immediately before execution, is well known. ʻEven since prison
discipline has been improved to such a degree that prisoners are, in
general, debarred from alcoholic drinks, the prohibition is still relaxed
in favor of one just about to die. Thus, the journals in reporting the
recent case of the Anarchists said,[1] that on the fatal morning, at the
instance of the sheriff, the assistant county physician went in and
asked the men if they cared for any stimulants. Parsons and Fischer
declined, but Engle said that port wine would suit his taste, and it
was supplied. He drank of it two or three times. Spies, who had
resumed his writing, expressed a wish for Rhine wine which was
brought from the nearest saloon, and of which he drank sparingly.

To multiply accounts or reports of this usual incident of an execution cannot be needful. A condemned man usually wishes for some
intoxicating liquor, and the executioner willingly assents. One reason
assigned for allowing him to stupefy himself with drink is that it is a
mercy to permit him to lessen his perception of the pain of dying;
another is that he can thus fortify himself with unnatural strength or
fortitude for the approaching ordeal.

Both these reasons are objectionable. In opposition to the first it
may well be said that if the pain incidental to the execution is an
essential part thereof, then the criminal has lawfully incurred it and
should be compelled to suffer it. If it is unessential, a proper narcotic
or anæsthetic should be given. In either case the resort to alcohol,

---

[1] New York Times, November 12, 1887.

as a means of stupefying the sufferer, argues a defect in the method
of execution. Moreover, if liquor given be enough to intoxicate the
condemned, he becomes drunk. Drunkenness is in itself an offense.
In the moral aspect the gross impropriety of sending a man into the
presence of his Maker intoxicated is too obvious to require comment.
This has in some instances been perceived by the condemned themselves. Dymond[1] relates, of the hanging of Allen Mair, that, after
the preliminary religious exercises had been concluded "a glass of
wine was brought to him, but he resolutely refused it, declaring that
he would not go into the presence of Almighty God drunk."

As to the second reason above mentioned for giving liquor, that it
may impart strength, this is unjustifiable, except, perhaps, in rare cases
where life must be prolonged by the use of stimulants, in order that
the final sentence may be carried into effect, as in cases where the
strength has been dangerously reduced by the loss of blood through
an attempt at suicide. Even then, if the resort to stimulation be
necessary, a hypodermic injection of some diffusive stimulant would
be more rapid and desirable. Again, liquor given under the pretext
of strengthening and encouraging the man to bear hanging is quite
as likely to strengthen and encourage him to resist, and many
instances of disorderly conduct by the condemned, at the gallows, are
doubtless to be explained as the effects of giving the man liquor.
Finally, the law regards intoxication, when an element in the commission of crime, as an aggrevation of the offense; why should it sanction
or treat leniently intoxication as an incident to a capital execution?

The next objection presented to your commission is the incidental
danger of an attempt by the condemned to commit suicide, and of
some subsequent horrible scene.

An attempt at suicide, made by cutting the throat, often fails because
the victim, either from lack of knowledge or from physical irresolu-
tion at the instant, severs only the windpipe instead of the jugular
vein. In cases of this kind, which are far from uncommon, the lesion
of the cartilage seriously weakens the resistance of the neck to the
fall, and the result may be that the fall completely separates head
from body. If so horrid a catastrophe does not occur, still the
mutilated appearance of the body is often repulsive and shocking to
an extreme. So it may be if any other mode of self-wounding is
employed. In the noted case of John C. Colt, who stabbed himself

---

[1] The Law on its Trial, p. 118.

to the heart during a few moments of privacy accorded to him just before the time set for the hanging; or in the recent case of the condemned anarchist who adjusted a small bomb in his mouth so that its explosion mutilated his head; if either had survived but a short time a shocking scene at the hanging would have been a natural result. Four instances are mentioned in which an attempt at suicide has added horrors to the scene which followed; also one case in which the wound which complicated the death was not given with suicidal purpose.

The execution of William Gordon, at Tyburn, on Wednesday, April 25, 1733,[1] is in point: "While under sentence, Gordon behaved very decently and gravely, and with an appearance of a real repentance, only that he loved company a little too much, when any freedom was given him; and in evidence of his sincerity, he received the blessed sacrament twice, once when he was at first under sentence, and again the morning he was executed, in company with two other of his fellow-sufferers. No sooner had he received this blessed viaticum, in pledge of eternal life, but going down stairs, and being conveyed unto his own cell, he cut his throat with a razor which had been privately given him. In two minutes one of the keepers, going in after him, found him all over bloody; then he took him out to a room in the press-yard, and there being by accident two surgeons within the jail, one of them sewed up his throat and put him in a condition of recovery and living to have the sentence of death executed upon him according to law. He denied that he had any design of murdering himself, but declared that he only by accident cut his throat a little, as he was cutting away his stock, which was too fast tied."

"The law," says Charles Spear,[2] "knows no bounds to its cruelty, for we have an account of the execution of a pirate in Boston, even after his attempt to commit suicide. It appears that he had been narrowly watched, but the sheriff leaving him for a moment, he seized the opportunity and attempted to take his own life. But, so barbarous and stern is the law that life must be taken by its own ministers while the wound was flowing fresh, and while life was almost extinct he was taken in a chair, placed under the gallows and cruelly murdered."

Moir says[3] that at the execution of Joseph Myers and James Sar

---

[1] Old Bailey Cases, vol. 4, p. 63.   [2] Capital Punishment, 11th ed., 1845
[3] Capital Punishment, p. 141.

gissòn, which took place at Leeds, September 10, 1864, a horrible scene
was enacted. Myers, after the commission of the murder for which
he was executed, attempted to commit suicide by cutting his throat.
"A short time previous to the execution," says a local paper, "attention
was directed to the wound in Myers' throat, and one of the wardens
placed a small plaster upon it. Unfortunately this was not sufficient. A few days before the execution Myers alluded to the state of
his throat, and said that if the executioner did not give him "another
yard of fall" he should not die, for he could breathe through the
wound. He showed to the person he addressed that he could actually
respire through the wound. The wound was in the middle of the
throat and the rope would necessarily come above it, so that there
was imminent danger of a horrible scene unless the place was securely
plastered over. The event showed that proper means had not been
taken to obviate this danger. The fall did not dislocate his neck
because of his weight, but *was sufficiently violent to tear open the wound*,
and a dreadful scene ensued. After one or two movements Myers
ceased apparently to struggle, and the attention of the executioner
was directed to Sargisson, who struggled violently and seemed to die
very hard. But after a minute had elapsed it was seen that Myers
was still alive, and that *breathing was going on through the wound in the
throat below the rope*. The dreadful occurrence caused an overpowering
feeling of horror; but after a consultation with the surgeon steps
were taken which resulted in the eventual fulfillment of the sentence;
but this was not accomplished until more than twenty minutes had
expired after the drop fell. Whether sensibility remained in the body
during the whole of that time it is impossible for us to say. Certain,
however, it is that the culprit breathed for that time, and that the
hoarse sound of the air rushing into the lungs was distinctly audible.
Most fortunate it was that the screen in front of the drop completely
concealed the bodies from the sight of the enormous crowd. We
shudder to think of what consequences might have been if the populace had seen what took place behind the screen."

It is narrated[1] that in Scotland, where the law invests the judges
with power to punish criminals in such manner as they may deem to
be proportionate to their offenses, one Ross, whose crime had been
attended with many aggravating circumstances, was sentenced to have
his right hand chopped off, then to be hanged till dead, the body to

[1] 3 Jackson's Newgate Calendar, p. 279.

be hung in chains and the right hand to be affixed at the top of the
gibbet, with the knife made use of in the commission of the murder.
The day appointed for putting the sentence of the law into force
being arrived, Ross walked to the place of execution, holding Mr.
Craig by the arm. Having addressed a pathetic speech to the populace, and prayed some time with great fervency and devotion, the rope
was put around his neck, and the other end of it being thrown over
the gallows, it was taken hold of by four chimney sweepers. The
criminal now laid his right hand upon a block, and it was struck off
by the executioner at two blows; immediately after which the chimney
sweepers, by pulling the rope, raised him from the ground. When
he felt the rope drawing tight, by a convulsive motion he struck the
bloody wrist against his cheek, which gave him an appearance too
ghastly to admit of description. The body was put into chains and
hung upon a gibbet, the hand being placed over the head with the knife
stuck through it. This took place at Edinburgh on January 8, 1751.

Your commission have met with many accounts of various shocking scenes which have occurred at the gallows. The strong and
general prejudice among cultured or high-minded persons against
executions by hanging has doubtless been fostered by the multitude
of accounts which have been published of such scenes which have
occurred, not necessarily connected with the death penalty, but
naturally incident to it when hanging is the mode. Hundreds of
such narratives might be found. Your commission here present a
limited selection arranged so as to illustrate certain causes which
have always tended to render an execution by hanging harrowing to
the feelings of the sensitive, demoralizing to the brutal, the force of
which would be much diminished by adopting the more humane and
private form hereinafter recommended. They are, *first*, resistance
or suffering by the offender; *second*, unskillfulness or brutal indifference of the executioner; *third*, misconduct of bystanders; *fourth*, sympathy of bystanders occasioned by the great age or other personal
circumstances of the condemned; *fifth*, complication of the process
caused by a supposed necessity of executing more than one person at
one time. Instances in which bad impressions have been produced
on persons where the criminal was a woman, or was disfigured or
mutilated under a recent wound, are elsewhere stated.[1]

The worst impressions are, according to experience, produced in

---

[1] Moir, Capital Pun., p. 138.

those cases in which the execution is not successfully carried out; when, for instance, the executioner, through his awkwardness, gives, at least apparently, unnecessary pain to the culprit ; this may occur in every mode of execution, even that by the guillotine. In these cases indignation against the authorities is manifested; the people cannot understand how the government should have the right of torturing the unfortunate man in such a horrible manner, and the prevailing feeling of compassion for the culprit extinguishes all respect for the law.

Many cases are chronicled of the resistance or suffering of the offender. It is related[1] that at the execution of Heald and Terry, "Terry was not to be restrained, and it was only from the utmost exertions of five or six men that he could be dragged to the drop and the rope forced over his head. During this he tore off his cap and at the moment when the platform sank, which put an end to the life of Heald, Terry made a spring and threw himself against the rail of the scaffold, got his foot over the edge of a beam, and caught the corner post with his arm, by which he supported himself ; and in this dreadful situation he continued for about a minute, till he was forced off by the executioner and launched into eternity with his face uncovered, a circumstance never, perhaps, known in the annals of a York execution.

At the execution of Samuel Mitchell,[2] he was not allowed to remain long on the scaffold, as he was tied up almost on the instant after he came up. After the drop fell he exhibited several times the appearance of feeling great pain, as he swung around twice, which was occasioned by the violence of the convulsive struggles he sustained.

The execution of Boyington is thus described :[3] " He walked to the scaffold with a firm and unwavering step. His whole soul had been steeled and nerved up, till the ministers of the law commenced robing him for death, and fixing the fatal noose. At that moment he cowered and sunk into the most abject desperation ; a more sudden and fearful transition, perhaps, was never witnessed. ' Is there no hope ? Must I die ?' were answered in the negative. The blood forsook his cheeks, despair was written in awful marks upon his ashy features, and a scene of horror ensued that beggars description. He dashed from the foot of the scaffold among the military. But he was easily

---

[1] Jackson's Newgate Calendar, vol. 7, p. 88.
[2] Id., p. 192.
[3] Spear's Capital Punishment, 11th ed., 1845.

secured. Then followed a scene of horror, which we pray may find no parallel hereafter in the execution of the laws. The hopeless agony of the criminal was displayed in obstinate resistance to the performance of the necessary duties of the agents of the law ; and even when at last suspended from the fatal cord, his desperate clinging to the life he had forfeited was shown by struggles to free his arms from the pinions and clutching at the rope. He succeeding in thrusting his hands between the rope and his throat, and thus, resisting and struggling to the last, died despairing, and for aught that human eye could see, impenitent. The last five minutes of his life were marked by a horror of dying, a prostration of energies, as remarkable as the sternness of nerve and reckless levity of carriage which had signalized him during the whole of the trial, and in the interval between condemnation and execution, up to that moment."

The same author says, that in the execution of Stephen M. Clarke, only seventeen years of age, for setting fire to a building in Newburyport, it was found necessary to force him from his cell and drag him to the scaffold, amidst a parade of soldiers and martial music.

Dymond[1] relates a horrifying scene which occurred at Newgate when William Bousfield was hanged, March 31, 1856. The wretched convict was a man of the lowest possible moral condition, and his conduct, while awaiting his sentence, was sullen and morose in the extreme. When the chaplain alluded to his crime, he would say : "Pray, don't talk about it, it is a horrid dream ;" and he persistently refused all religious consolation. On the Saturday preceding the day (Monday) of execution, whilst sitting with a turnkey in the condemned cell, Bousfield suddenly darted forward, and placed his head on the fire, his chin resting on the top bar. He was dragged off, but frightfully disfigured. During that night and the whole of Sunday, means were applied to reduce the inflammation, and make him less hideous in appearance ; but he took no notice, and refused all nourishment except a little milk and wine. On Monday morning he was apparently in a most exhausted state. His face was bound in cloths, and he presented a spectacle most fearful to behold, as he was seated, or rather sustained, in a chair by the attendants. No inducement could make him stand ; and two men supporting his body, and two his legs, he was borne to the

---

[1] The Law on its Trial, p. 160.

foot of the scaffold. Here he was again seated in a chair, and thus carried to the drop, where he sat crouching, a pitiable exhibition of the most abject terror and weakness. Some person had frightened Calcraft by sending him a letter threatening to shoot him when he appeared to perform his task. Having hastily adjusted the cap and rope, he ran down the steps, drew the bolt, and disappeared. For a second or two the body hung motionless; then, with a strength that astonished the attendant officials, Bousfield slowly drew himself up, and rested with his feet on the right side of the drop. One of the turnkeys rushed forward and pushed him off. Again the wretched creature succeeded in obtaining foothold, but this time on the left side of the drop. The sheriffs, horrified, sought for Calcraft and with difficulty the chaplain forced him to return. He thrust the miserable wretch off once more. For a fourth time Bousfield raised himself and obtained foothold. Again he was thrust off, and Calcraft, *throwing himself upon the suspended body by main force strangled him at last.* Meantime the crowd were greatly excited; their shouts and execrations arose with a fearful clamor around the gallows, and cries of "shame," "shame," "murder," "murder," greeted the ears of the representative of British justice. No wonder that there are men found who urge that these scenes should be hid by the prison walls from the public gaze. The institution could not stand any more such shocks to its reputation as that which the incidents of Bousfield's execution occasioned.

Another serious objection is the casualty often resulting from the unskillfulness or indifference of the executioner. In the execution of James Smith,[1] on board the sloop-of-war Parthian, December 26, 1809, for murder, about half an hour before nine A. M., Smith was brought, in custody of the provost-marshal, on board, in order to undergo the sentence. At a quarter past nine he ascended the scaffold, where he did not remain more than five minutes before the fatal gun fired. By some accident or inattention on the part of those whose province it was to make fast the rope on board, the coil was suffered to slip, and the unfortunate culprit was precipitated with great velocity to the water's edge; he was again drawn up, and after hanging the usual time, the lifeless body was lowered into a boat.

At the execution of Buranelli,[2] April 30, 1855, through the improper adjustment of the rope, his sufferings were prolonged for fully five

[1] Jackson's Newgate Calendar, vol, 1, p. 84.
[2] Dymond, The Law on its Trial, p. 194.

minutes. The wretched man was fearfully convulsed, his chest heaved, and it was evident that the struggle was a cruel one. The mob became indignant, and shouted forth execrations against the barbarous spectacle. But death came at last.

Arnot[1] states that at a Scotch execution, the executioner mangled the condemned so shockingly in the discharge of his duty that he was next day turned out of office.

Charles Spear[2] gives the following painful account of an execution of two brothers: "James died without a struggle, but, melancholy to relate, the rope by which Alexander was suspended, broke, and he was precipitated to the pavement, a distance of nearly forty feet. He fell with the side of his head on his own coffin, which was broken and rebounded off it a few feet. He was instantly carried in (supposed to be dead) by two officers of the jail. The executioner, also dressed in white, with the part that covered his face daubed over with black, by the assistance of a ladder, soon put another and a stronger rope over the block, and with some difficulty again raised the drop, in doing which, the unfortunate culprit, then suspended, was pushed as much as possible to the one side and lowered a little further. In about twenty minutes from the time he fell, to the astonishment of the assembled multitude, Alexander again appeared and walked out on to the drop more firmly than before, answering to the prayers of the clergy. He took his place, and the signal being given the drop was again slipped but rested on the shoulder of James, who was pushed aside, and Alexander was launched into eternity, but not suddenly. The board slowly moved down, sliding along James' body. The knot of the rope had shifted round the chin of Alexander, and he suffered dreadfully for several minutes. His whole body was convulsed; during the strangulation he several times put his feet to the wall, and pushed himself from it with great force; his clothes burst open so that his naked breast was seen, and the cap not being altogether over his face, blood was seen flowing from the wound which he had received on the cheek in the fall. The feelings of the beholders cannot be described, they were most agonizing. At length, his hands fell, his body was seen to stretch, and he hung motionless alongside his brother."

Bovee[3] states that in March, 1865, at the execution of Atkinson, a

---

[1] Scotch Criminal Trials, p. 138.
[2] Capital Punishment, 11th ed., 1845, p. 47.
[3] Christ and the Gallows, p. 213.

collier at Dunham, the rope broke and the criminal fell alive to the
ground. After half an hour's delay the poor bruised wretch was hanged
the second time. Again at Stafford, at the execution of Collier, in
August, 1856, the rope broke and the man fell to the ground and had
to be rehanged. Other similar scenes have not been uncommon. He
considers that such horrors are just as likely to occur when executions are conducted in private as when there are openness and
publicity.

A very recent illustration of this occurred in Oakland, California, as
late as January 7, 1888 where a man named Nathan B. Sutton, was
hanged for murder. It is thus described in a daily paper :[1]
 "After his speech, Sutton stepped back. He betrayed no emotion
while his arms and legs were being pinioned, and when the noose was
being arranged, said coolly "Let me have the necktie." The black cap
was drawn over his face, and the trap was sprung at 12.16 o'clock
The drop was nearly five feet, and the fall was so great that *the man*
neck was torn by the rope, the spectacle prompting many of those present t
avert their faces. In fifteen minutes the body was lowered into th
coffin."

The injudicious and often unfeeling conduct of bystanders, althoug
in part done away by the restriction as to their presence, is anothe
serious objection.

A remarkable circumstance happened to one Gow, at the place o
execution.[2] His friends, anxious to see him out of his pain, pulle
his legs so forcibly that the rope broke and he dropped down ; o
which he was again taken up to the gibbet, and when he was des
was hung in chains on the banks of the Thames.

Of the execution of Harriet Parker, it is related[3] that her condu
in prison exhibited the most intense remorse for her crime. Th
chaplain declared — and he was not one to be easily deceived — th
he had seen no such evidence in any other case under his care.
earnest, humble penitence. When the time for her execution can
she joined with the chaplain and attendants, all deeply affected,
singing a hymn. Then she received the sacrament, and that solen
rite was hardly over when the hangman entered to pinion her. Su
mitting quietly to that operation, she set forth to the scaffold, t
whole company again joining in a hymn. But the mob got impatie

---

[1] N. Y. World of January 8, 1888.
[2] Jackson's Newgate Calendar, vol. 2, p. 204.
[3] Dymond, The Law on its Trial, p, 142.

for the devotions of the prisoner had somewhat delayed her appearance., Thirsting for their horrid treat, as the condemned one appeared at the door leading to the drop a perfect tornado of yells, shrieks and curses fell upon her ear. The sight and sound of that crowd of demons were too much; the frightened creature fell fainting into the arms of the attendants and was carried forward and hung in a state of insensibility.

The same writer records that at the execution of Sarah Chesham, convicted of poisoning, some delay occurred, the officials having difficulty in persuading Chesham to ascend the scaffold. She was led up, or half carried at last, and placed beside her companion in misery. After the execution, and whilst the bodies where still hanging, Calcraft came through the crowd to a public house, accompanied by some of the gaol turnkeys. The crowd, with loud cheers, rushed after him, and each rivaled the other in attempts to exchange a friendly word with the executioner. When the people had somewhat dispersed, I returned into town and watched their conduct from the windows of the hotel. The grand business of the morning accomplished, the day was evidently to be devoted to debauchery. Every public house was full ; obscene language could be heard on every side, and as the day wore on drunkenness got the ascendant, and I saw young country lads and girls clinging in reeling groups together, or even rolling in the gutters of the public streets.

The like scenes occur to-day outside the prison walls when an execution takes place in any of our large cities.

But one of the most distressing cases in which the execution by hanging becomes revolting is in the case of very aged criminals. Allan. Mair[1] whose refusal to take wine on the scaffold has already been mentioned, was sentenced, in 1843, at eighty-four years of age, to be hanged.

After the trial the utmost effort was made by the authorities of the town to obtain a remission of the sentence, and a petition was forwarded to the Secretary of State, but the answer returned was that "the law must take its course." As the hour approached he became very restless, and on leaving the cell was very much agitated and wept bitterly. He had previously declared his resolution not to walk, and had accordingly to be supported by two men who led him into the court-house. During the customary religious exercises he wept much, the tears

---

[1] Dymond's The Law on its Trial, p. 118.

streaming through his bony fingers when he pressed them to his face, and every now and then he wrung his hands. He seemed to take little notice of what was passing around him, his mind being evidently absorbed in thinking of his approaching execution. Here the executioner, who was singularly attired in a light jacket and trousers, seamed with red and black, and a huge black crape mask, entered the room, on seeing whom Mair started back, and every limb appeared to quiver with the intensity of his excitement. The executioner then advanced to pinion him, but Mair shrunk away, evidently alarmed at his approach. On the rope being passed round his arms he complained that it was hurting him. "Oh, dinna hurt me," said he, "dinna hurt me.' I'm auld — I'll make nae resistance. An' oh, when I gang to the gibbet, dinna keep me lang, just fling me off at ance." After some difficulty he was pinioned, and the mournful procession being formed, he was led out between two officers to the scaffold. On emerging from the court-house, and when the gibbet and the immense crowd met his gaze, he held down his head and groaned piteously, lifting up his hands and ejaculating, "Oh, Lord; Oh, Lord." He was instantly led to the drop, but he declared he was unable to stand, and as he had expressed a resolution to address the multitude, a chair was brought for him. On sitting down he appeared to gather additional strength and resolution, and addressed the crowd with a mixture of asseverations and curses. Then there was prayer. The executioner then put the cap on the old man's head, adjusted the rope and placed the signal handkerchief in his hand. At this time he was sitting on the chair on the drop, and although the cap was drawn down over his face he continued muttering his anathemas against all who had connection with his trial. He was then desired to rise from the chair, in order that it might be removed, but he replied that he could not, wept piteously, and while in the act of exclaiming, "May God be ——," the fatal bolt was withdrawn, and the wretched old man, uttering a heavy groan, was launched into eternity. For a moment he raised one of his hands, which had not been properly pinioned, to the back of his neck, seized the rope convulsively and endeavored to save himself, but his grasp instantly relaxed, and after struggling violently for some time he ceased to exist.

Where there are several executions by hanging at one time, the result is often ghastly and horrible, and the danger of some sad or demoralizing scene is increased. Such cases are not infrequent. In the execution of the Lincoln conspirators, four, one of them a woman, were included. It is said that in a case of arson and murder involving rebellious Indians, about twenty-five years ago, thirty-seven persons were hanged at one time; and that this is the largest number which has been put to death in this way. A recent instance of several hanged, at once is that of the anarchists last fall at Chicago. The following account was published at the time. After relating the preliminary proceedings, the narrative proceeds:[1]

"Then there was a click, a rattling crash, and in a second four white heads hung on a level with the scaffold. Parsons' body hung motionless for a minute. The drop was about four feet six inches, and the shock to the medulla of the vertebræ of the neck paralyzed motion. Then some grotesque struggles supervened, and the lithe frame of the anarchist swayed frightfully at the end of the rope. His neck was not broken, and the horrors of a death from strangulation occurred. The folds of the shroud heaved and twisted agonizedly, and the less hardened lookers on pitied the dying anguish of the sufferer, as his chest heaved in the involuntary efforts of the lungs to obtain air. The convulsions continued a few minutes. They suddenly ceased. All was still, and Parsons' soul went thence to test the question whether 'humanity' is the God-head of the universe.

"Engel's fall must have broken his thick, short, bull neck. The heavy body severely tried the cord when the drop occurred, but the sheriff's test of strength had been wisely conducted. The physicians report that the neck was not broken, but that speedy death ensued from shock to the spinal cord. Be the facts what they may, he suffered less than the others when his flight through space was checked.

"Fischer hung limp for a few seconds, and then some weak convulsive throbbing partially disarranged the white face cap. A horrible spectacle was presented by the instantaneous glimpse I was enabled to obtain of the anarchist's mouth. The tongue protruded and was clenched between the teeth. A purple shade suffused the lower portion of the face, and the horror of a dying agony by strangulation was apparent. One of the doctors who held a thumb and finger to the wrist pulse mercifully swung the body around so that the hideous sight was hidden. Fischer's fingers contracted violently a few times, then all was still, and the blood engorged hands hung limp.

"Spies' body went through some ghastly contortions at the noose's end. The description of the hanging at Dublin jail in the old Irish

---

[1] N. Y. Herald, Nov. 12, 1887.

poem, where the final struggles of the victim was termed the 'Kilmainham minuet,' was recalled by the scaffold dance of Nina Van Zandt's lover. His head wagged toward the people on the floor as if imploring aid. The struggle grew sharper and sharper until finally, when the spectators began to wonder if they would ever cease, the form straightened out, and, so far as human vengeance is concerned, the spirits of the murdered policemen were appeased."

The next point of consideration on this subject is the possibility of attempts at resuscitation.

A journalist who lately questioned the usefulness of the inquiry entrusted to your commission, denies all possibility of resuscitation of a man who has been hanged, and urges, in favor of adhering to that method, his belief that no man has ever escaped the gallows. Your commission have not thought it useful to inquire whether such a resuscitation is possible, or has ever, in fact, occurred. They submit that a general belief exists among the unlearned that such resuscitations are possible by gross collusion between the officers of the law and the condemned man, and have in some cases occurred, and your commission urge that such a belief, however unfounded in fact, casts a doubt over the administration of the penal law which it would be well to dispel. In support of the statement, not that resuscitations from judicial hanging have occurred, but that many persons have believed them possible, the following assertions are made by a well-recognized legal authority.[1]

Some unsuccessful attempts have been made to preserve the lives of criminals condemned to suffer the punishment of the law, by the introduction of a tube, or making an opening into the windpipe below the place where the rope is usually fixed; when the neck is not broken, nor the weight of the body very great, the experiment in all probability might prove successful. Professor Richardson says he was informed by a respectable surgeon in the Austrian army, that he had saved the life of a criminal by performing the operation of laryngotomy a short time previous to the execution. A similar experiment was tried on one Gordon, a butcher, executed at the Old Bailey, in the early part of the last century. The body having hung the usual time, was removed to a neighboring house where a surgeon waited to receive it, to use every means calculated to restore animation; he opened his eyes and sighed, but soon expired; the want of success was attributed to his great weight.

---

[1] Forsyth's Medical Jurisprudence, p. 252.

The same writer,[1] speaking of persons found hanged by accident or with felonious or suicidal effect, advises the following treatment to be followed in such cases. The same measures recommended for restoring drowned persons are necessary here, with the addition, however, of opening the jugular veins, or applying cupping-glasses to the neck, which will considerably tend to facilitate the restoration to life, by diminishing the quantity of blood contained in the head, and thereby taking off the pressure from the brain. The quantity of blood to be abstracted in this manner, unless in persons of a very plethoric habit, need scarce exceed an ordinary teacupful, which will generally be found sufficient to unload the vessels of the head, without weakening the powers of life.

One of the popular journals narrates a number of traditions which have given currency to a suspicion that resuscitations have occurred.

There are many instances on record in which the punishment of suspension by the collar has failed, either through some peculiarity in the neck of the individual, or a want of tact in the hangman. More than six centuries ago, if old records are truthful, Juetta de Balsham, convicted of harboring thieves, was sentenced to be executed. She hung for three days, revived and was pardoned, as a phenomenon who had somehow or other overmastered the gallows.

There is the authority of Obadiah Walker, master of New College, Oxford, for a story that a Swiss was hanged thirteen times over, every attempt being frustrated by a peculiarity in the wind-pipe which prevented strangulation. We are not told whether the thirteenth time was successful or whether justice was merciful at last.

Ann Green was hanged at Oxford, for infanticide, in 1650; her legs were pulled and her body struck with soldiers' muskets, in accordance with a barbarous custom sometimes adopted of making assurance doubly sure. Nevertheless she survived, after hanging some considerable time. Her body was given up for dissection. The surgeon observed faint signs of life, and attended her instead of anatomizing her, and in thirteen hours she was able to speak. She remembered nothing distinctly of what had occurred, but seemed to herself to have been in a deep sleep. The crown pardoned her; she married, and became the mother of a family, and her husband forgave her the errors of her past life, possibly for a kind of celebrity which

---

[1] Forsyth's Medical Jurisprudence, p. 255.

the singular episode had brought to her. Other examples, of a more or less analogous kind, are told as follows:

A woman, name unknown, was hanged in 1808. She came to herself after a suspension for the prescribed period, not by slow degrees, but suddenly.

John Green experienced an ordeal something like that of Ann Green. After being hanged at Tyburn, his body was taken to Sir William Blizzard, the celebrated surgeon, and while lying on a table in the dissecting room he displayed signs of life, and effectually recovered.

A female servant of Mrs. Cope, at Oxford, convicted of some penal offense, was executed in 1650. After hanging an unusually long time she was cut down and fell heavily to the ground. The shock revived her, but the unfortunate wretch was effectually hanged the next day.

Margaret Dickson, a century and a half ago, was convicted of concealment of birth, and was subjected to the last penalty of the law. Her body, after hanging on the gibbet at Edinburgh, was cut down and given to her friends. They put it in a coffin and drove off with it in a cart six miles to Musselburg. Some apprentices rudely stopped the cart and loosened the lid of the coffin. This let in the air, and the air and the jolting together revived her. She was carried indoors alive, but faint and barely conscious; a minister came to pray with her and she effectually recovered. No mention of collusion occurs in this narrative, although some of the incidents seem to point that way. Margaret lived many years, had other children born to her, and was familiarly known in Edinburgh, where she lived by selling salt, as "half-hanged Maggie."

The last mentioned case seems corroborated later[1] as follows:

Of the execution of Margaret Dickson, convicted of infanticide, it is related that, "after execution, the body was cut down and delivered to her friends, who put it into a coffin and sent it in a cart to be buried in her native place; but the weather being sultry, the persons who had the body in their care stopped to drink at a village called Pepper-mill, about two miles from Edinburgh. While they were refreshing themselves, one of them perceived the lid of the coffin move, and uncovering it the woman immediately sat up, and most of the spectators ran off with every sign of trepidation. It happened that a person who was then drinking in the public house had recol-

---

[1] Jackson's Newgate Calendar, vol. 2, p. 155.

lection enough to bleed her, and in about an hour she was put to bed, and by the following morning she was so far recovered as to be able to walk to her own house." By the Scottish law, which is in part founded on that of the Romans, a person against whom the judgment of the court has been executed can suffer no more in future, but is thenceforward totally exculpated; and it is likewise held that the marriage is dissolved by the execution of the convicted party, which, indeed, is consistent with the ideas that common sense would form on such an occasion. Mrs. Dickson then, being convicted and executed as above mentioned, the king's advocate could prosecute her no farther, but he filed a bill in the High Court of Justiciary against the sheriff for omitting to fulfill the law. The husband of this revived convict married her publicly a few days after she was hanged, and she constantly denied that she had been guilty of the alleged crime. She was living as late as the year 1753. This singular transaction took place in the year 1728.

A story of this sort was circulated by some of the daily papers, relating to the recent execution of August Spies. It was contradicted as follows:[1]

"The story circulated to the effect that efforts were made to resuscitate the body of August Spies, after his execution, is positively denied by Dr. George Thilo, who examined the body after it was delivered to the friends, and pronounced life to be totally extinct. This afternoon Dr. Thilo said: 'When the body was first brought to Mueller's undertaking establishment, some of the people present thought they perceived unusual warmth in the corpse, and I was sent for. I made a careful examination, and was soon convinced that death had intervened, and that any attempt at revivification, by galvanic battery or any other means, would be useless, and so I informed those present. There was no attempt whatsoever to restore life.' There is but one case known to medical science where a man judicially hanged has been resuscitated. That case occurred in Austria a few years ago. The criminal hanged for fifteen minutes, and when cut down was turned over to the physicians for experiment. Within five minutes from the time he was cut down, or within twenty minutes from the time the drop fell, the body was on the operating table, and a powerful galvanic current applied. The neck was not broken, and after a great deal of labor in producing artificial respiration, and the

---

[1]New York Tribune of November 23, 1887.

electricity being constantly applied, the subject revived, but in a state of wild delirium. From this he never recovered, and in twenty-four hours he died. Now, restorative agents were used in this case, within twenty minutes after the hanging, while in the Spies case it was three hours before the body was brought to the undertaker's."

The following is an extract from a personal letter received by the chairman of the commission from a well-known journalist:

"There is in this city a man who, while serving in the war as a member of a company in the New Jersey Volunteers, and while acting as one of 'Sherman's Bummers,' in Georgia, on a foraging expedition, was, with six others, captured by Shelby's guerillas and hung to a tree. When discovered, all seven were senseless and black in the face. All were cut down, but despite the efforts made but one was resuscitated, and that is the man living here to-day. There are several of his comrades living who are witnesses to the circumstances being true as related. * * * The rope slipped so that he was not immediately strangled, but while it prolonged his agony it probably saved his life. There is a lump on his throat yet, caused by the knot, and it was twenty years ago. The strain on his neck totally destroyed the sight of one eye."

But a much more serious objection exists to employing the gallows in the execution *of women.*

There is no need of expatiating at length on the grave, deep-seated objection which exists in the public mind against inflicting the death penalty upon a woman. This objection is so strong and widespread that it often secures a verdict of acquittal, or of a lighter grade of crime than that charged, as in a case in Connecticut not many years ago, where a woman accused of murder by poisoning was found guilty in the second degree only. It induces pardons in cases where pardons are without proper grounds. It feeds and keeps alive for years a spirit of hostility to the law which commands so unseemly a sacrifice. Your commission believe that the public opposition to the death penalty, in the case of women, when intelligently analyzed, will be found to be not so much an objection to the infliction of the penalty itself, but an execration of the barbarity, the increased inhumanity, the heightened shock to the feelings, when the usual incidents of hanging as the mode are imagined as applied to a female. Let the anticipation be that a judicial death will be inflicted in private, and in an instantaneous way, and the mode will be freed from fruitless appeals for sympathy, from struggles and from incidents intervening

when accident or unskillfulness aggravate the scene. It may be
confidently expected that the earnestness of this special objection will
be diminished, especially if ample means are taken to preclude the
disaster of involving an unborn child in its mother's death. It is not
so much to the *execution* of women as to the *hanging* of women that
the general objection is addressed. How well-founded this objection
has been in past years may be better understood from a few of the
numerous accounts which exist than from any extended remarks of
your commission thereon.

The account given[1] of the execution of Catharine Hayes, convicted
of the murder of her husband, states that it was customary, when
women were burnt for petit treason, to strangle them by means of
a rope passed around the neck and pulled by the executioner; so
that they were dead before the flames reached the body. But this
woman was literally burnt alive; for, the executioner letting go the
rope sooner than usual, the fire burnt fiercely around her, and the
spectators beheld her pushing the faggots from her, while she rent
the air with her cries and lamentations. Though other faggots were
thrown on her, she survived amidst the flames for a considerable time,
and her body was not perfectly reduced to ashes in less than three
hours. This singular mode of her death became as much the subject
of public conversation has her life had been; and many letters were
published in the newspapers on the occasion. One party insisted that
she had been thus executed in consequence of private orders from the
people in power, founded on the shocking circumstances of aggravation which attended her crimes; while other people contended that
the sheriff had given orders that the law should be thus rigorously
executed. But a third party insisted that neither of these was the
fact, but that the flames reached the hands of the executioner, he was
compelled to let go the rope for his own safety, and indeed, this seems
the most probable opinion.

Says a prominent writer:[2] "The execution of women was for a
long period a source of great difficulty to the home office, and this
was more especially the case when conviction took place for infanticide. Many causes will suggest themselves to the reader why the
public mind should view the execution of a woman with especial
horror and disgust. The resistance offered to the application of
capital punishment in cases of infanticide manifested itself both upon

---

[1] Jackson's Newgate Calendar, vol. 2, p. 124.
[2] Dymond, The Law c its Trial, p. 97.

the trial and after, if, as rarely happened, a capital conviction took place.

And he suggests[1] that the execution of two young and weakly persons would be attended with equally distressing circumstances, which would only perpetuate the feelings of disgust which such events at the same prison created.

So, of the execution of Mary Gallop,[2] it is said that on the night before her execution she was removed from the county gaol, in which she had been confined, to the city gaol, where the gallows was to be erected. The near approach of the event brought on an attack of fainting, and it became evident that the scene on the scaffold would be a most painful one. So, truly, it was. She was carried senseless to the drop, and thus strangled before the eyes of thousands collected to behold this splendid demonstration of the vindicated dignity of British law.

Of the execution of Martha Browning it is related :[3] "The scene on the gallows disgusted even the vile crowd that came to enjoy the spectacle. The hangman, with some roughness, pulled the culprit's cap from her head, and threw it on the ground to replace it by the one that was to cover her face. Then he seemed to fumble a long time about her throat whilst adjusting the cord ; and, apparently through some mismanagement, the wretched girl's struggles lasted for fully ten minutes after the fall of the drop, the crowd, meantime, yelling furiously in condemnation of the brutal exhibition."

Again, of the execution of Sarah Harriet Thomas, the account is that[4] :   "When the hour arrived for her to die, the governor of the gaol entered the condemned cell to lead her to the scaffold. She refused to move; expostulations and threats to employ force were fruitless. At length the governor ordered half a dozen turnkeys to bring her out. A terrible scene ensued. Against six stalwart men the hapless prisoner struggled in vain ; but her shrieks rang through the prison—'I'll not go; I'll not go ;' and she was dragged into the press yard. There the hangman pinioned her, and for a while she became more calm. A few soothing words from the governor induced her to walk quietly to the foot of the ladder leading to the drop. Then again she resisted. Two turnkeys carried her up the

[1] Dymond, The Law on its Trial, p. 132.
[2] Id., p. 138.
[3] Id., p. 139.
[4] Id., p. 159.

ladder, her appalling screams falling on the ears of the people outside. 'Oh, don't hurt me; don't hurt me,' she cried, seizing him
with her pinioned hands. The executioner was moved, for though a
hangman, he was a father, and as he said, 'the thought of his own
girls came over him.' He tried to comfort the terrified creature—
'No, no, my poor girl, I'll not hurt you.' Then he rapidly adjusted
the rope, bade her to cry 'Lord have mercy on me,' and as she
uttered the name of the All Merciful One, cut her forever from the
mercy of earth."

A horrible scene[1] took place at the execution of a murderess at
Appenzell, December 3, 1849. She had to be dragged by several men
from the prison to the market-place, and could not be executed till
after a struggle which lasted almost an hour and a-half. Finally the
head of the unhappy woman was fastened to a long pole by the tresses
of her hair and forcibly torn from the body, which was secured to
the ground.

The Daily Telegraph (a London newspaper) thus alludes[2] to such
a spectacle: "Now and again the law has been allowed to take its
course, and a wretched woman has been dragged from the jail to the
scaffold, struggling with the wardens, biting and clawing them, shrieking and kicking, and plunging, till the hangman's assistants have
forced her into the chair beneath the beam, and sent her out of the
world with the clothes half torn off her back." These disgusting
accompaniments characterized the execution of the women, Ashford
at Exeter, Holt at Chester and Sarah Thomas at Bristol.

In June 1863,[3] Alice Holt was committed for trial for poisoning her
mother. The accused was pregnant. In consequence of this, her
trial was postponed from the summer to the winter assizes; meantime
her confinement took place. Had she been tried in the summer, her
pregnancy would have been allowed to act as a bar to execution; but
by the postponement that difficulty was overcome and Alice Holt was
hanged. The scene upon the scaffold was more than usually distressing. The wretched woman, weak and faint, was kept several minutes waiting for the drop to fall, owing to some difficulty with the
bolt. Meantime her cries to the hangman to "make haste," excited
the pity and sympathy of the crowd who had come to witness the
revolting spectacle.

---

[1] John Macrae Moir, on Capital Punishment, p. 143.

[2] Bovee, Christ and the Gallows, p. 213.

[3] Dymond, Law on its Trial, p. 157.

Moir[1] makes the forcible suggestion: Attention must be claimed to the peculiar circumstance which occurs when a pregnant woman is sentenced to death. In this case the law orders the execution to be delayed. Have legislators duly weighed what effect the protracted agonies of the mother have upon the unfortunate child?

The difficulty and uncertainty in determining the question of pregnancy in a capital case is illustrated by the case of Mary Wright[2] after the verdict of guilty had been rendered and sentence of death pronounced:

Mr. Sydney Taylor moved to stay the execution, on the ground of the prisoner's pregnancy, and the court ordered a jury of matrons to be impaneled to try that plea. The jury of matrons gave, as their verdict, that they "Did not find the prisoner pregnant of a *quick* child." As the forewoman of the jury delivered the verdict, in the words of the ancient formula, the sharp ear of the humane advocate detected an emphasis on the word "quick." This was enough for him. He said he thought, from the manner in which the verdict of the jury of matrons was given, that they did not intend to negative the pregnancy, but only to deny that the child had "quickened."

To this Mr. Baron Bolland replied: "I have done all that the law empowers me to do; I don't see what more I can do."

"The law," said Taylor, "gives your lordship a discretionary power to stay the execution, even in case of murder, if there should be a danger of any fatal mistake. I am sure I need not press upon your humane mind the propriety of acting upon that discretion, if there should be the remote danger of confounding innocent life in the punishment of guilt. Surely it is more safe to act upon the opinions of medical men than upon those of unlearned women."

The judge rejoined: "At present I can do nothing more; but I will take the subject into consideration."

The next morning, upon the sitting of the court, the learned judge, addressing Mr. Sydney Taylor, informed him that he had taken into consideration the suggestion he had made in relation to the finding of the jury of matrons, in the case of the prisoner Mary Wright; that in the course of the previous evening he had communicated with three eminent practitioners in Norwich, the result of which communication was that he had determined to stay the execution.

Mr. Taylor asked whether his lordship meant to stay the execution

[1] Capital Punishment, p. 195.
[2] Dymond's Law on its Trial, p. 68.

to any precise time or, generally, to which Mr. Baron Bolland replied "generally."

A short time previous to the next assizes an event happened which fully established the fallacy of the old women's verdict and confirmed the propriety of the learned baron's humane discretion; for Mary Wright was delivered of a child, thus demonstrating that, but for her counsel's humane intervention, one of the most horrible spectacles possible to conceive might have taken place before the gaze of the people of Norwich.

Another case[1] was that of Charlotte Harris, arrested and tried for murder of her former husband. She was found to be pregnant, and respited accordingly; but after the birth of the child a disposition was manifested by the executive to carry out the sentence. Again public opinion rose against the law. It was essentially a women's question, and the humanity of England's daughters revolted at the barbarity of detaining a miserable creature for months in suspense as to her fate, and then, after she had given birth to her infant, tearing it from her arms and strangling her like a dog. Some 40,000 women appealed by memorial to their queen. Harris was reprieved, and it has since become an established principle that no woman sentenced under such circumstances shall ever be hanged.

The case of Roxalana Druse, executed in Herkimer county on the twenty-eighth day of February, 1887, is too recent and too fresh in the memory of all, to justify any detailed statement with reference to it. The protests which came up from all parts of the State against her execution, and the public excitement in reference to her case, showed the existence of a widespread and deep-seated sentiment against the hanging of women.

CHANGE OF PRESENT METHOD ADVISABLE.

Fourth. Your commission are satisfied, in view of the above stated objections to the present method of execution by hanging, that the time has come when a radical change should be effected. It is only after a long and exhaustive examination of the subject that they have arrived at this conclusion, and while the general voice of the press has strongly urged for some time past the propriety of such a change, yet it is only after a careful weighing of the reasons and objections thereto that a correct result can   had. The deprivation of life is

---

[1] Dymond, Law on its Trial, p. 157.

in itself, the most serious loss which any human being can suffer.
To aggravate that loss by any method which even incidentally
increases the pains of dissolution, or renders the execution of the law
more terrible, is justifiable only upon the argument as to its deterrent
effect. As already shown, that has been tried for ages without success.

The Constitutional Prohibition of Cruel and Unusual Punishments.

Fifth. Your commission have paid due attention to the fifth section
of article 1 of the Constitution of this State, forbidding the infliction
of "cruel and unusual punishments." Under the various statutory
forms in which this prohibition has appeared during the past two
centuries, it has been the subject of much judicial comment.

"Difficulty would attend the effort to define with exactness the
extent of the constitutional provision," said Mr. Justice Clifford,
delivering the opinion of the United States Supreme Court[1] "which
provides that cruel and unusual punishments shall not be inflicted,
but it is safe to affirm that punishments of torture, such as those mentioned by the learned commentator referred to (Blackstone), and all
others in the same line of unnecessary cruelty, are forbidden by that
amendment to the Constitution."

Your commission entertain no doubt, however, that a punishment,
to be prohibited by the Constitution must be *both* unusual *and* cruel.
A punishment which is cruel, but not unusual, would not be prohibited,
nor, on the other hand, would one which is unusual, but not cruel.
Certainly, in one sense, hanging is cruel, but not unusual, and on the
other hand, there are other methods which, while unusual, are
not cruel.

The people in the present day are opposed to anything like a spirit
of vengeance in the execution of the law, and while the methods may
accomplish the result desired, yet at the same time to aggravate the
horror of death by subjecting the offender to additional intense
physical pain, is contrary, not only to the humanity of the age, but to
the intent of the law itself.

Sixth. Your commission are firmly convinced that if the criminal
could be put to death in a certain and efficacious manner, the purpose
of the law would be achieved equally well as if the terrors of death
were enhanced by the infliction of pr longed physical torture before
the end was finally accomplished.

---

[1] Wilkerson v. Utah, 99 U. S., 135.

Various suggestions have been made as to the means of accomplishing such a result. One has been the injection of a violent and sudden poison, such as prussic acid, by means of the hypodermic needle, into the body of the condemned, which is open to the very serious objection that the use of that instrument is so associated with the practice of medicine, and as a legitimate means of alleviating human suffering, that it is hardly deemed advisable to urge its application for the purposes of legal executions against the almost unanimous protest of the medical profession.

Proposed Substitution of Electricity for Hanging, and Reasons Therefor.

Perhaps the most potent agent known for the destruction of human life is electricity. Death, as a result, is instantaneous upon its application. The application may be made without the slightest injury to the officers charged therewith; the place for its infliction may be strictly private, and at the same time its certainty is beyond a doubt.

It is the duty of society to utilize for its benefit the advantages and facilities which science has uncovered to its view.

One objection urged against the use of electricity is the shock which the lay mind is prone to think must, of necessity, be incidental to its use. Even if a shock were experienced, it is difficult to understand how it could be as objectionable as the dropping from the scaffold, in the method which now obtains. But an electric shock of sufficient force to produce death cannot, in fact, produce a sensation which can be recognized.

The velocity of the electric current is so great that the brain is paralyzed; is indeed dead before the nerves can communicate any sense of shock. Prof. Helmholtz estimates the interval necessary for nerve communication with the brain at one-tenth of a second. Prof. Tyndal estimates that an electric discharge occurs in one hundred thousandth of a second, or ten thousand times more rapidly than nerve transmission.

Upon this subject, and also upon the general adaptability of electricity, Prof. Elihu Thompson, of Lynn, Mass., in reply to a communication from your commission, states:

"The strength of current which will produce death depends largely upon the nature of its source, and t on the direction of its passage through the body, and, besides, varies greatly with the peculiar individual constitution of the subject, other things being equal. In most cases death seems to be the result of nerve exhaustion and asphyxia, and in others may be due to rupture of blood vessels or injury to the valves of the heart, as a consequence of violent contraction, under the enormous stimulus of powerful currents. Broken or interrupted currents or alternating currents, the waves of which are abrupt in character, are without doubt the most powerful in injurious effects upon the animal system. I think it would be quite possible to construct a small machine to give the requisite currents by induction from a small storage or other battery current; or a small machine run by hand or by a water motor might be employed, which machine would be designed for the most powerful physiological effects, the nature and strength of current being selected in accordance with this object. The machine would not, I think, be very expensive. I should think that from one to two hundred dollars would amply cover its cost.

"I should hardly be inclined to favor passing the current through the arms by a metal armed chair, because in the first place, there might be difficulty in getting the subject to take hold; and in the next place, some constitutions show a wonderful power of resistance to currents passing transversely.

"The most certain way to produce death would be to pass the current down the spinal cord from the crown of the head, as by the sudden application of wet surfaces or sponges. The result would be, I think, with a sufficiently strong current of the proper character, a painless extinction of all the faculties; and the current being kept on for a little time, would result in such complete nervous exhaustion as to forbid any possibility of resuscitation by any means whatever.

"I am of the opinion that no more humane treatment could be devised; for I believe there could in no case be any pain felt.

"In all cases of severe electric shock which have come to my notice, and in which unconsciousness has resulted with recovery afterward, the subject has testified to remembering nothing up to the point of regaining partial consciousness, and that no pain was felt."

Upon this same subject Mr. Thomas A. Edison writes:

"The best appliance in this connection is, to my mind, the one which will perform its work in the shortest space of time, and inflict the least amount of suffering upon its victim. This, I believe, can be accomplished by the use of electricity, and the most suitable apparatus for the purpose is that class dynamo-electric machinery which employs intermittent currents. The most effective of these are known as 'alternating machines.' The passage of the current from these machines through the human body, even by the slightest contacts, produces instantaneous death."

It has been the good fortune of a member of your commission to witness a number of experiments with electricity as a means of destroying animal life, and, at the request of the commission, Dr. George E. Fell, of Buffalo, under whose supervision they were conducted, has made an extended report, from which we quote the following:

"In the month of July, 1887, there was conducted a series of experiments calculated to throw considerable light upon the powerful and injurious effect of electricity upon animal life. The authorities of the city of Buffalo, N. Y., had determined to rid the city of the numerous curs roaming the streets. To reduce their sufferings to a minimum, the agent of the Society for the Prevention of Cruelty to Animals recommended that electricity be applied as the death-dealing agent. The experiments were conducted at the improvised dog pound prepared at old police headquarters. The canines were quartered in one room; adjoining this was an entry which communicated with a third room, in which the electrical apparatus was located. This consisted of a common pine box, lined with zinc, and connected with one pole of the electric light current for that portion of the city. When in use the box was partially filled with water. Connected with the electric light wire, representing the other pole, was an ordinary dog muzzle, supplied with an iron or copper bit, which was inserted into the mouth of the canine. The animal being placed in the box, the switch making the circuit was turned, causing the apparent instantaneous death of the animal. Only in exceptional cases were any movements noted after the current was made.

"The results obtained by experiments conducted in this manner leaves the subject just where public opinion would place it, viz., 'that electricity will kill quickly.' However, to ascertain how quickly and thoroughly requires further demonstration.

"The heart may rightf lly be considered the center of function, and in the execution of ɩ inals by the legalized hanging process, is always examined to ascertain when death ensues. In favorable cases it is known that the heart m. beat from six to ten minutes, and in some cases it has been known ɩo beat from fifteen to thirty minutes before death. For the purp se of ascertaining the effect of electric light current on the actio ɩ of the heart, the operation

of opening the thorax of an animal under forced respiration was
made. With the operation satisfactorily performed, the. heart and
lungs may be observed in action, viz., the heart beating and the
lungs contracting and expanding as in life.

"While the operation is not new to physiologists, still the effects
upon the movements of the exposed heart, by the passage of an
electrical current which might be applied in the execution of criminals, I do not believe has been frequently noted or the operation often
performed. That the ordinary electric light current used in these
experiments is sufficient to cause instantaneous death of a human
being, is inferred from the many accidental deaths produced by such
means. To witness the effect produced upon the heart in action is a
demonstration which cannot be questioned, and offers a positive
answer to what may have been inferred, and has already amounted to
a foregone conclusion.

"To those favoring electricity as the proper agent in the execution
of criminals, a demonstration of this character serves to make them
more positive and less liable to be influenced by those whose investigations into the subject have been only superficial. Those opposed to it
from the standpoint of uncertainty of action, it leaves without a
foundation upon which to base their opinion. Prior to these experiments, I held the view that electricity might prove the best agent for
executing criminals; after they were made I enthusiastically supported
it as the only agent which this age had any right to use for this
purpose.

"But to refer to the experiments: A fair sized dog was placed under
the influence of cloroform, an incision was made in the trachea, in
which a tube connecting with foot bellows, and supplied with suitable
valve for respiratory purposes, was attached. Respirations were then
kept up by these artificial means. The chest walls (thorax) were then
removed so that the heart and lungs were exposed to view; the dog
was then placed in the zinc-lined box, the muzzle put on, the forced
respiration kept up until just before the current was made. The
heart was beating as in life, but the insta⸍ ᵗ the circuit was made it
ceased its action and became a mere mᴀs ᵓ quivering flesh; not the
least resemblance to a rhythmical movement was observed after the
current was made. Many citiz ₃ present at the operation can testify
to the above; in fact the demᴄᵤstration as to suddeness of stoppage
of the heart exceeded all a ticipation. The interference with all
function was electrically instᴀ ntaneous, death ensued from electric

shock, the ordinary conditions of dying were absent; nothing could be more sudden.

"This first experiment, although eminently satisfactory in its results, was made under conditions the most unsatisfactory; the rooms were full of men hurrying to and fro; the dogs were being led to their fate, and no suitable place was provided to operate. This, and observations connected with another series of investigations, led to a second demonstration which was made under more favorable conditions at the electric light works on Wilkeson street, Buffalo. This operation was conducted with greater care; instead of the muzzle with the bit attached to make one pole of the circuit, a piece of wire line was placed in the mouth of the dog, and wound around the nose. The zinc box was used as before; chloroform narcosis was produced and the thoracic walls removed. The heart was beating rhythmically; on making the circuit it instantly ceased to beat. The current was quickly turned off and forced respiration kept up with the view of bringing the heart again into action; this was entirely unsuccessful. The result demonstrates that if the current used is sufficiently powerful, attempts at resuscitation in the case of a criminal executed by electricity would certainly fail.

"In this second experiment it was also noticed that an attempt to respire was made by the animal after the current was made. This undoubtedly indicated that the respiratory center in the brain (medulla) had not completely lost its susceptibility to impressions; and that, through the want of oxygen in the blood and center noted, the effort to breathe was formulated. This has an important bearing upon the apparatus to be used in executions, inasmuch as it indicates that the poles should be arranged to pass the current through the centers of function in the brain. Upon physiological grounds, also, this is indicated. Even without this refinement of precision in the apparatus, as has been shown in this last experiment where the current was not passed directly through the functional brain center, the sudden stoppage of the heart would indicate that electricity offers the most rapid agent in producing death that we have at our command.

"The mere estimates of the difference in the speed of the electric, as compared with the nervous current, would further show that our senses could not interpret or apprehend the passage, or that death produced by such means would be absolutely painless to the culprit. From observations which are generally accepted, it may be stated that nervous force travels at a rate of from one to two hundred feet per second, while the electric passes at a rate of not less than two hundred thousand feet per second, or about one thousand times as rapid. From these observations, the following deductions may be drawn:

"*First.* That death produced by a sufficiently powerful electric current is the most rapid and humane produced by any agent at our command.

"*Second.* That resuscitation, after the passage of such a current through the body and functional centers of the brain, is impossible.

"*Third.* That the apparatus to be used should be arranged to permit the current to pass through the centers of function and intelligence in the brain."

Your commission are satisfied that the appliances for an execution by electricity can be made extremely simple.

All that would be essential would be a chair, with a head and foot-rest, in which the condemned could be seated in a semi-reclining position; one electrode would be connected with the head-rest, and the other with the foot-rest, which would consist of a metal plate. The expense of such a chair would not exceed fifty dollars. If the current of electricity is supplied from the electric light wires, there would be but slight expense necessarily incurred to make the connection from the chair with the wires on the outside. If, however, it is deemed best to have an independent wire running directly from the electric light plant to the place of execution, there would be the additional expense of constructing an independent line for that purpose, which would depend somewhat on the length of the line, varying from $250 to $500. If, however, it is deemed best to have an independent appliance (consisting of an alternating machine, or such a machine as that suggested by Professor Thompson, as above set forth, which would furnish an electric current of sufficient power entirely independent of any outside communication), the expense would be between $250 and $500.

The cost of maintenance of either of the foregoing plans would be merely nominal. After the plant is once established, the expense of conducting an execution would be infinitesimal. Your commission are of the opinion that the most advisable plan would be to establish places of execution in the State prisons located at Auburn, Sing Sing and Dannemora, and that at each place there should be established an independent plant, which could be operated independently of any outside communication, and which would be ready for use at all times. In addition to this, a connection could be had with electric-light wires, so that under all circumstances and contingencies there could be no failure of a sufficient current for the purpose of carrying the death penalty into effect.

The expense of such a double appliance would not, in the opinion of your commission, exceed the sum of $1,000 for each of the three places, and when once established, it would be in the nature of a permanent structure, involving substantially no expense in keeping it in repair.

SEVENTH. Before coming to any conclusion in regard to the duty committed to it, your commission issued a circular containing the following questions:

"*First*. Do you consider the present mode of inflicting capital punishment, by hanging, objectionable? Please give the reasons for your opinion.

"*Second*. Were you ever present at an execution, and, if so, will you kindly state details of the occurrence bearing on the subject?

" *Third*. In your opinion, is there any method known to science which would carry into effect the death penalty in capital cases, in a more humane and practical manner than the present one of hanging? If so, what would you suggest?

" *Fourth*. The following substitutes for hanging have been suggested to the commission. What are your views as to each?

. 1. Electricity.

2. Prussic acid, or other poison.

3. The guillotine.

4. The garrote.

"*Fifth*. If a less painful method of execution than the present should be adopted, would any legal disposition of the body of the executed criminal be expedient, in your judgment in order that the deterrent effect of capital punishment might not be lessened by the change? What do you suggest on this head?"

This circular was sent to the justices of the Supreme Court and to the county judges, district attorneys and sheriffs throughout the State, and also to a large number of the members of the medical profession. Some 200 answers were received to the circular. Of these, about eighty were in favor of retaining the present method of inflicting capital punishment, the rest were generally in favor of a change. Eighty-seven were either decidedly in favor of electricity, or in favor of it if any change was made. Eight expressed a preference for poisons; five for the guillotine; four for the garrote; seven for various other methods of taking life, and eight were non-committal. The justices of the Supreme Court who responded were about equally divided in opinion between retaining the present system and electricity. One correspondent favored hanging for men, and death by electricity for women. Another suggested that hanging be retained in aggravated cases, and electricity used where there were mitigating circumstances, the selection of either of these means of inflicting the death penalty to be in the discretion of the judge. Many of those who were inclined to oppose any change, were in favor of trying electricity, if any change should be made. The objections stated to electricity were, mainly its supposed uncertainty, and also the supposed difficulty of managing it so as to avoid danger to the officers of the law while inflicting death on the convict. The following extract from the letter of N. E. Brill, M. D., of New York, who is strongly opposed to hanging, and favors the guillotine as a substitute, fairly presents the objections raised to this method of capital punishment:

 " *Electricity.*— The consideration of expense in procuring dynamos of sufficient power, and I do not believe they would be of any service unless they were of at least fifty (50) horse-power, is one which must be considered together with that of the power to work the dynamos and which some of the counties of the State could hardly afford. Again, the transportation of the same to the various sites of execution, would be an increased burden. Of course, the condemned could be brought to the instrument, but that would be inflicting additional torture and mental suffering on him by causing an agonizing *expectant attention.* But my greatest objection to electricity is that its action is a very variable one. The following from the *Philadelphia Ledger,* March 29, 1886, is reported, and is but a repetition of a similar accident occurring in this city some time previous, where two men working on the same line of a Brush arc light were suddenly stricken down by an unlooked for completion of the electrical circuit; the one being immediately killed and the other escaping with but a burn of the hand and wrist ' Very little is known about the effects of strong currents of electricity such as a lightning stroke or the current from an arc lighting dynamo, upon the physical organism. People who receive shocks from such a current are generally killed, as Daniel Cough was in this city last Saturday, and Myers Patterson at Lynchburg, Monday, yet others almost unaccountably escape. A workman at Liverpool was handling a crane, which came in contact with an electric lamp, and the current passed through his body. He was made insensible by the shock, but soon recovered, although the intensity of the current was such that his hand was burned and the sole of his foot badly charred. His stocking was also burned, but his shoe was uninjured.'

"You are aware that lightning may strike an individual and not kill; and no dynamo ever made can produce a shock as great, both in intensity and quantity, as nature's own manufacture. In fact, the atmospheric influences in reference to the human body, acting as a conductor, must be taken into consideration and guarded against. Yet they are beyond our control, for the same amount of electrical discharge acts differently on different occasions. In fact, some persons have a special power of repelling the baneful influences of such a discharge applied to their bodies. This must, of course, reside in special differences in their morphological structure, so that the effect of an electrical shock applied is a very indefinite one, and cannot be depended upon to produce more than a momentary convulsion, with or without loss of consciousness in some, and death in others. If lightning do not always kill, surely we cannot expect death to result from artificial electricity."

The following extract from the *Lancet* appended to a letter from one of the justices of the Supreme Court, who is in favor of adhering to the present method, is also presented :

"Electricity is another agent suggested. We doubt the possibility of applying this agent so as to destroy life instantly. We confess that, looking at the matter all around, we incline to think that hanging, when properly performed, destroys consciousness more rapidly, and prevents its return more effectually than any other mode of death which justice can employ. It is against the bungling way of hanging we protest, not against the method of executing itself. That is, on the whole, the best, we are convinced."

These and similar objections have been carefully considered by your commission. We cannot think that, from the fact that in accidental encounters with electricity it sometimes happens that the person exposed does not get the full force of the current, and thus escapes death, it follows that there is any uncertainty as to a fatal and immediate result where the electric force is directly and scientifically applied to a vital part of the body. We have satisfied ourselves, from careful consideration and inquiry, made of experts in electricity, that the objections made are unfounded. The opinions of some emi-

nent authorities on the subject of electricity have already been quoted.
We think there is no practical difficulty in constructing an electrical
apparatus which can easily and safely be managed, and which will be
absolutely certain in its working, and will effect the instantaneous
and painless death of the convicted criminal. We quote a few of the
expressions on this subject contained in the answers to our circulars :

Dr. J. H. Chittenden, of Binghamton, writes: "Electricity would
produce instantaneous death if properly applied. I would prefer it
to the drop or weight."

Dr. Lewis Balch, of Albany, (who is in favor of retaining the
present mode of inflicting capital punishment), says of electricity:
"I believe this could be used. It would, however, require a skilled
workman to have charge of the batteries, to insure their proper
working. Various modes of working could be easily suggested.
The death would be instantaneous, perfectly painless, with no
distortion."

J. Henry Furman, of Tarrytown, writes : "I believe electricity
would fulfill the conditions humanity and civilization demand, to wit,
instantaneity of death and integrity of the body. I think it not
superfluous to state, electric force, if generated in a similar manner
to that used in producing electric light, and in the same or in diminished quantity, would, if properly applied, produce immediate and
painless death without mutilation of the body. I would suggest a
metallic chair with conducting plates adjustable to opposite sides of
those portions of the body where the brain and spinal cord lie ; also,
that the executioner be invisible to the condemned person."

A. P. Jackson, M. D., of Oakfield, N. Y., who rather favors retaining
the present mode, says of electricity: "It is a most admirable substitute, probably the best known to science, fulfilling all the indications
in the most humane, practical and painless manner."

E. J. Kauffmann, M. D., Licentiate of the Faculty of Physicians and
Surgeons, Glasgow, Scotland, writes as follows:

"Death from lightning is instantaneous, painless and absolutely
certain. We can produce artificial lightning by means of an electric
battery, and hence the same admirable results in such cases, as would
be produced by lightning itself in probably a space of time not cover-
ing more than the one hundredth part of a second. Therefore, the
use of electricity as a means of execution is scientific, devoid of all
barbarism, instantaneous and complete.

"A further factor, which would recommend its use, may be drawn from this fact, that those discharges which, from their intensity, kill most readily, leave fewest and least marks of external injury."

Charles A. Leale, M. D., President of the New York County Medical Association, says: "Electricity is rapid and certain; yet requires special apparatus and one familiar with its use."

Dr. M. J. Lewi, of Albany, says: "Electricity, if properly utilized, would, to my mind, prove the most humane and speedy method of execution."

Hon. Edward A. Mahar, who has had experience in the management of the electric lights in the city of Albany, writes: "In my judgment, electricity can be used with certainty of fatal effect."

William T. Plant, M. D., of Syracuse, says: "Electricity — this way, is certainly worthy of careful consideration. It has the merit, if it is a merit, of instantaneousness. I think that, with proper apparatus and with proper skill, the operation may be made certain and safe from mishap; but only actual trial can determine whether it is best."

Dr. L. M. Pratt, of Albany, says: "In my opinion, the most humane and practical manner to carry into effect the death penalty would be by electricity."

Judge Vann, of Syracuse, writes: "Electricity is not only the least painful and repulsive, but, also, the quickest, most certain and most easily administered."

Judge Westbrook, of Amsterdam, writes: "Death by electricity, when properly applied, would be instantaneous and painless."

J. C. Weber, Superintendent of the Brush Electric Light Company of Buffalo, writes: "I have witnessed several accidental deaths by electricity, each of which were instantaneous, and in neither case was there any visible trace of the agent of death on the face of the victims. In view of this fact, I cannot but feel that the present advanced state of knowledge of electric force should afford the most humane and, at the same time, the most effective method of inflicting the death penalty."

The fifth question contained in the circular above referred to was not very generally answered by those who responded to the circular. A great proportion of those who did answer this question, however, were in favor of surrendering the body of the criminal to medical men for dissection, and opposed to delivering it to the friends, at least for public burial. The following answer to this question from the

Hon. Lucius N. Bangs, of Buffalo, states very clearly and concisely the argument in favor of such law:

"*Fifth.* As the life of the criminal is forfeited to the State, the body should be also, the State to make such use of it for scientific purposes as would be decent and proper. Such use, while considered as no part of the punishment, would be deterrent in its tendency on criminals. Generally, I would say, the duty that falls upon the State is *to deprive the criminal of life for the safety of the public.* It is not to *torture* the criminal by way of *punishment.* The duty of the State is, therefore, best performed when it applies the speediest method of extinguishing life. All criminals for execution should be sent to one place where the most perfect methods could be made available. After final sentence, intercourse with the criminal should be absolutely prohibited, except by those having a duty to perform in relation to him. The *time* of execution should be indefinite, except that it should be between two fixed dates, and the public should *never* be advised of such actual time of execution. After final sentence the criminal should drop absolutely out of public sight and consciousness."

Alfred Ludlow Carroll, M. D., of New Brighton, writes: "As regards the fifth question, my personal observation has led to a firm conviction that further legislation is needed to increase the deterrent effect of any (even the present) mode of capital punishment. To the most dangerous of the criminal class, the scaffold bears no associations of disgrace; it is rather a heroic culmination of a career of proud and daring defiance of law, almost to be emulated by the survivors; and the pageant obsequies permitted after an execution often constitute a *quasi* apotheosis of crime and invite the imitative ambition of less distinguished evil-doers. But the majority of this class entertain an insuperable antipathy to disfigurement of the dead body, even to the most delicately conducted *post-mortem* examination; and an extension of the law's visitation in this direction, involving the abolition of funeral display, would, I believe, be commonly more dreaded than the death penalty itself. I would suggest, if it be consonant with other provisions of the law, that a statute be enacted giving the bodies of executed criminal to medical colleges for dissection. Nothing save an overstrained sentimentalism could be opposed to such a measure, socially considered, and I feel confident of its preventive efficacy in an enormous number of depraved minds."

Upon this subject the attention of your commission has been called to a law of the State of New Jersey, which was enacted March 3, 1882, and which is as follows:

"CHAPTER XLII.

"A Supplement to an Act Entitled 'An act for the Punishment of Crimes.'

"Be it enacted, by the Senate and General Assembly of the State of New Jersey, that it shall be unlawful to expose to public view the body of any person who shall have suffered the infliction of the death penalty, either in this State or in any part of the United States, for the crime of murder, after such body shall have been delivered from the custody of the sheriff; and it shall be unlawful to have any public funeral or gathering in connection with the burial of the body of any such offender.

"2. And be it enacted, that prior to the delivery of the body of any such person, upon whom the death penalty shall have been inflicted, to the relatives or friends, or to any person or persons, or to any association, the party or parties so applying for possession of such body shall file with the sheriff, having custody of such body, a bond in the sum of one hundred dollars, with two sufficient sureties, which bond shall be forfeited to the county in case of a violation of the provisions of this act; and if no application for such body be made, and bond filed, on or before the day on which the death penalty is inflicted, the sheriff may deliver such body to any surgeon or medical college for dissection, or he may cause such body to be otherwise disposed of.

"3. And be it enacted, that any person offending against the provisions of this act, and being convicted, shall be deemed and adjudged to be guilty of a misdemeanor, and be punished by a fine not exceeding two hundred and fifty dollars or imprisonment at hard labor not exceeding six mont'   r both."

In case the Legislature should not feel inclined to adopt the recommendation of your commission hereafter made on the subject of the disposal of the bodies of convicted murderers, we earnestly recommend that some provision be made similar to the law of New Jersey above quoted, to prevent the scandal of public funeral ceremonies over the remains of those who have suffered the death penalty for crime.

Several answers to our circular were devoted to the discussion of the propriety of abolishing capital punishment altogether, and some very able arguments in favor of such abolition have been forwarded. As this subject was not referred to your commission, we have paid no attention to it in our report.

Your commission have not appended to this report the numerous letters received in answer to the circular above mentioned, having given above the substance of some of the more important of them, and not being willing to increase the length of the report, which is necessarily somewhat voluminous.

· *Eighth.* One point remains to be considered by your commission — the subject of the deterrent effect of capital executions. It has purposely been inserted at this part of the report in order that the objections to the present, and the advantages of the proposed new method, might be placed side by side for the better enlightenment of the intelligent reader.

And first, it is said, in favor of the deterring effect of the execution by hanging, that it is a degrading and revolting system of death, that criminals dread it on that account, and that the very fact that such death is by no means instantaneous or painless, invests it with a wholesome dread by the criminal classes. A careful examination of the statistics of crime show that such effect has been greatly magnified. There has been no marked diminution of capital offenses since hanging has existed as a method of punishment. True, it is in every sense both a degrading and revolting means of death, and, to a certain degree, has a deterrent effect. But the criminal classes who are most prone to commit capital offenses are usually the most ignorant and brutal in the community. Devoid of religious sentiment, they are none the less superstitious and, strange as it may seem, are often more concerned as to what will happen to the body after death than as to their future spiritual existence. Among the ignorant, and even those who are utterly destitute of a belief in a future state, this dread especially exists. Very many bravos who will, without flinching, walk from th⸗ ". to the scaffold, and who are certainly very indifferent as to the infliction of death itself, would hesitate long to commit crim⸗ involving its application if they were certain that after execution their bodies were to be cut up in the interest of medical science. One of the principal reasons why at the present time the punishment of death by hanging appears to have so little weight in preventing the recurrence of the crimes for which it is inflicted, arises from the fact that too often the body of the criminal after death is handed over to his relatives and friends and treated by them as that of a martyr. The most disgusting scenes of this character have occurred, especially in the city of New York. After an execution has been duly performed with all the solemnity of the law, the friends of the deceased, his companions in crime and his sympathizers in its commission, having procured the body from the sheriff, indulge in the most drunken and beastly orgies. Eulogies of the deceased are pronounced as if he were a martyr instead of an executed criminal. His evil deeds are glorified into acts of heroism. And, so far from the punishment inflicted operating as a deterrent, the very boldness with which he marched from the cell to the scaffold is extolled as an act of heroism and an evidence of courage and valor. "He was game to the last" has been many a ruffian's eulogy.

Now if, instead of this, the execution were to take place in private, in presence only of the necessary officers of the law to ensure its due and proper infliction, and to preserve a proper record thereof, and immediately thereafter, a *post-mortem* examination were to be made of the body, and the latter were to be then delivered to medical men for dissection, all interest in the criminal would cease practically with his sentence. As his life is forfeited to the State, there seems to be no good reason why his body should not equally be the subject of forfeit; and your commission are decidedly of opinion that this would produce a far more effective result in diminishing crime than under any circumstances can now be accomplished by the present course pursued by the law with that end in view.

Another suggestion which your commission make is, that instead of the execution, as at the present time, taking place in the jail or prison of the particular county in which the offense was committed, a State prison should be designated as the place for its infliction, and immediately after sentence the criminal should be there conveyed without delay and kept until the sentence be carried into effect. The result of this would be: *First.* The lessening of the chance of any escape or rescue. *Second.* That sympathizing friends would not, as at the present time, on the day of an execution, gather in crowds around the jail where it takes place, and while unable to see what transpires, evince their sympathy for the condemned in a manner alike discreditable to public decency and dangerous to the public peace. *Third.* That instead of the sensational reports of the execution which always appear on the same day or the day following in the public prints giving a detail of the agonies and struggles of the dying wretch, a simple statement would be substituted to the effect that the sentence of the law had been duly carried into effect. It is true that the provisions of the Penal Code (§ 507) wisely and properly restrict the persons present, excluding all except the jury and officials necessary to enforce the law and preserve evidence of the due and proper infliction of the sentence. But the jury are often composed of representatives of the press, who are thus enabled to chronicle with painful fidelity every detail of the horrible scene which is then reproduced in the public prints chiefly as sensational matter. The result is that the execution, instead of operating as a deterrent, creates with many a vicious and morbid appetite for the disgusting description, and has been known even to stimulate others to the commission of crime. Your commission are far from recommending any legislation which may even indirectly tend to curtail the liberty of the press; especially because it is to the latter great credit is due to its fearless exposure of the evils attending the present system. But on the other hand they are satisfied that a restriction of the details, such for instance, as already exists in regard to the publication of evidence in proceedings for divorce, would not only meet with the hearty approval of the press itself, but greatly conduce to the moral and deterrent effect of the execution itself.

NINTH. Your commission respectfully present the following recommendations:

First. That the present method of inflicting the death penalty be abolished, and, as a substitute, that a current of electricity, of sufficient intensity to destroy life instantaneously, be passed through the body of the convict.

Second. That every such execution take place in a State prison, to be designated by the court in its judgment and death warrant, and that the time of the execution be not fixed by the court, except by designating a period within which it must take place.

Third. That immediately after the execution a post-mortem examination of the body be made by the physicians present, and the remains be then handed over to the medical profession for further dissection, or be buried without ceremony in the prison cemetery or grave-yard, with sufficient quicklime to ensure their immediate consumption.

Fourth. That the public accounts of the execution be limited as regards its details.

C

Lastly. Your commission, pursuant to the direction contained in the statute creating them, respectfully submit the foregoing to your consideration, and annex hereto, as part of their report, a proposed act, which they believe will render effective the changes they have suggested.

All of which is respectfully submitted,

ELBRIDGE T. GERRY,
MATTHEW HALE,
ALFRED P. SOUTHWICK,

Commission.

Dated ALBANY, *January,* 17, 1888.

AN ACT to provide for the proper infliction of the death penalty and to amend the existing provisions of law relative thereto.

The People of the State of New York, represented in Senate and Assembly, do enact as follows: .

SECTION 1. Section four hundred and ninety-one of the Code of Criminal Procedure of the State of New York is hereby amended so as to read as follows:

§ 491. When a defendant is sentenced to the punishment of death, the judge or judges holding the court at which the conviction takes place, or a majority of them, of whom the judge presiding must be one, must make out, sign and deliver to the sheriff of the county, a warrant stating the conviction and sentence, and appointing the week within which the sentence must be executed. Said warrant must be directed to the agent and warden of the State prison of this State designated by law as the place of confinement for male convicts sentenced to imprisonment in a State prison in the judicial district wherein such conviction has taken place, commanding such agent and warden to do execution of the sentence upon some day within the week thus appointed. Within ten days after the issuing of such warrant, the said sheriff must deliver the defendant, together with the warrant, to the agent and warden of the State prison therein named. From the time of said delivery to the said agent and warden, until the infliction of the punishment of death upon him, unless he shall be lawfully discharged from such imprisonment, the defendant shall be kept in solitary confinement at said State prison, and no person shall be allowed access to him without an order of the court, except the officers of the prison, his counsel, his physician, a priest or minister of religion, if he shall desire one, and the members of his family.

§ 2. Section four hundred and ninety-two of said Code of Criminal Procedure is hereby amended so as to read as follows:

§ 492. The week so appointed must begin not less than four weeks and not more than eight weeks after the sentence. The time of the execution within said week shall be left to the discretion of the agent and warden to whom the warrant is directed; but no previous announcement of the day or hour of the execution shall be made, except to the persons who shall be invited or permitted to be present at said execution, as hereinafter provided.

§ 3. Section five hundred and three of said Code of Criminal Procedure is hereby amended so as to read as follows:

§ 503. Whenever, for any reason other than insanity or pregnancy, a defendant sentenced to the punishment of death has not been executed pursuant to the sentence, at the time specified thereby, and the sentence or judgment inflicting the punishment stands in full force, the Court of Appeals or a judge thereof, or the Supreme Court or a justice thereof, upon application by the Attorney-General or of the district attorney of the county where the conviction was had, must make an order directed to the agent and warden or other officer in whose custody said defendant may be, commanding him to bring the convict before the Court of Appeals, or a General Term of the Supreme Court in the department, or a term of a Court of Oyer and Terminer in the county where the conviction was had. If the defendant be at large, a warrant may be issued by the Court of Appeals or a judge thereof, or by the Supreme Court or a justice thereof, directing any sheriff or other officer to bring the defendant before the Court of Appeals, or the Supreme Court, at a General Term thereof, or before a term of the Court of Oyer and Terminer in that county.

§ 4. Section five hundred and four of said Code of Criminal Procedure is hereby amended so as to read as follows:

§ 504. Upon the defendant being brought before the court it must inquire into the circumstances, and, if no legal reason exists against the execution of the sentence, it must issue its warrant to the agent and warden of the State prison mentioned in the original warrant and sentence, under the hands of the judge or judges, or of a majority of them, of whom the judge presiding must be one, commanding the said agent and warden to do execution of the sentence during the week appointed therein. The warrant must be obeyed by the agent and warden accordingly. The time of the execution within said week shall be left to the discretion of the agent and warden to whom the warrant is directed; but no previous announcement of the day or hour of the execution shall be made, except to the persons who shall be invited or permitted to be present at said execution as hereinafter provided.

§ 5. Section five hundred and five of said Code of Criminal Procedure is hereby amended so as to read as follows:

§ 505. The punishment of death must, in every case, be inflicted by causing to pass through the body of the convict a current of electricity, of sufficient intensity to cause death, and the application of such current must be continued until such convict is dead.

§ 6. Section five hundred and six of said Code of Criminal Procedure is hereby amended so as to read as follows:

§ 506. The punishment of death must be inflicted within the walls of the State prison designated in the warrant, or within the yard or inclosure adjoining thereto.

§ 7. Section five hundred and seven of said Code of Criminal Procedure is hereby amended so as to read as follows:

§ 507. It is the duty of the agent and warden to be present at the execution, and to invite the presence, by at least three days' previous notice, of a justice of the Supreme Court, the district attorney and the sheriff of the county wherein the conviction was had, together with two physicians and twelve reputable citizens of full age, to be selected by said agent and warden. Such agent and warden must, at the request of the criminal, permit such ministers of the gospel, priests or clergymen of any religious denomination, not exceeding two, being of full age, to be present at the execution; and in addition to the persons designated above, he may also appoint seven assistants or deputy sheriffs, who may attend the execution. He shall permit no other person to be present at such execution, except those designated in this section. Immediately after the execution a *post-mortem* examination of the body of the convict shall be made by the physicians present at the execution, and their report in writing, stating the nature of the examination so made by them, shall be annexed to the certificate hereinafter mentioned and filed therewith. After such *post-mortem* examination the body shall then be delivered by the agent and warden for the purposes of dissection to some public hospital or incorporated medical college within this State; or such body shall be interred in the grave-yard or cemetery attached to the prison, with a sufficient quantity of quick-lime to consume such body without delay; and no religious or other services shall be held over the remains after such execution; and in no case shall such remains be delivered to any relative or other person whatever. No account of the details of any such execution, beyond the statement of the fact that such convict was, on the day in question, duly executed according to law at the prison, shall be published in any newspaper. Any person who shall violate or omit to comply with any provision of this section, shall be guilty of a misdemeanor.

§ 8. Section five hundred and eight of said Code of Criminal Procedure is hereby amended so as to read as follows:

§ 508. The agent and warden attending the execution must prepare and sign a certificate, setting forth the time and place thereof, and that the convict was then and there executed, in conformity to the sentence of the court and the provisions of this code, and must procure such certificate to be signed by all the persons present and witnessing the execution. He must cause the certificate, together with the certificate of the *post-mortem* examination mentioned in the preceding section, and annexed thereto, to be filed within ten days after the execution, in the office of the clerk of the county in which the conviction was had.

§ 9. Section five hundred and nine of said Code of Criminal Procedure is hereby amended so as to read as follows:

§ 509. In case of the disability, from illness or other sufficient cause, of the agent and warden to whom the death warrant is directed, to be present and execute said warrant, it shall be the duty of the principal keeper of said prison, or such officer of said prison as may be designated by the superintendent of State prisons, to execute the said warrant, and to perform all the other duties by this act imposed upon said agent and warden.

§ 10. The superintendent of State prisons shall, on or before the first day of January, one thousand eight hundred and eighty-nine, cause an electrical apparatus, suitable and sufficient for the purposes specified in this act, to be constructed and placed in each of the State prisons of this State, together with the necessary appliances for the execution of convicted criminals, under the provisions of this act.

§ 11. Nothing contained in any provision of this act applies to a crime committed at any time before the day when this act takes effect. Such crime must be punished according to the provisions of law existing when it is committed, in the same manner as if this act had not been passed; and the provisions of law for the infliction of the penalty of death upon convicted criminals, in existence on the day prior to the passage of this act, are continued in existence and applicable to all crimes punishable by death, which have been or may be committed before the time when this act takes effect. A crime punishable by death, committed after the beginning of the day when this act takes effect, must be punished according to the provisions of this act, and not otherwise.

§ 12. All acts and parts of acts inconsistent with the provisions of this act are hereby repealed.

§ 13. This act shall take effect on the first day of January one thousand eight hundred and eighty-nine, and shall apply to all convictions for crimes punishable by death committed on or after that date.

Made in the USA
Las Vegas, NV
25 September 2022

55925124R00056